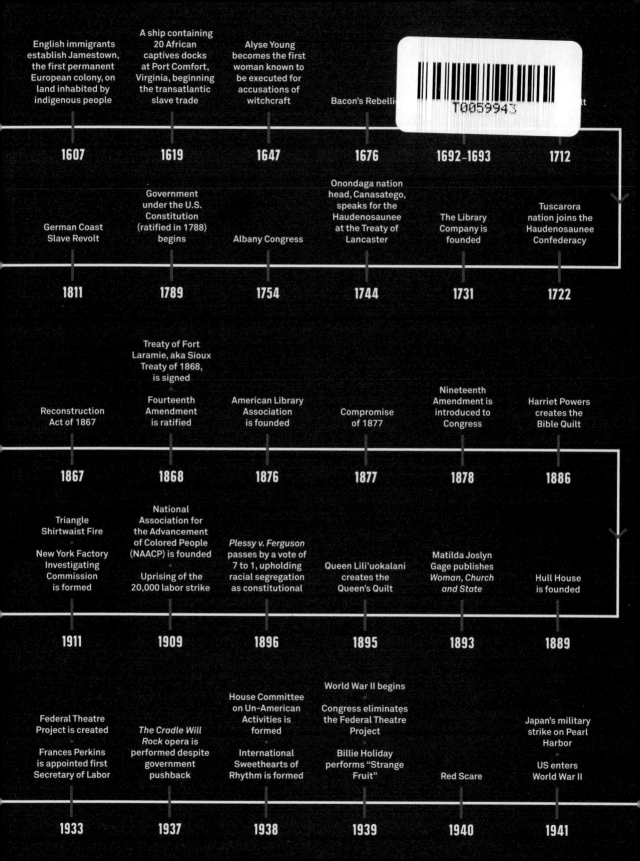

English immigrants establish Jamestown, the first permanent European colony, on land inhabited by indigenous people

A ship containing 20 African captives docks at Port Comfort, Virginia, beginning the transatlantic slave trade

Alyse Young becomes the first woman known to be executed for accusations of witchcraft

Bacon's Rebellion

1607 **1619** **1647** **1676** **1692–1693** **1712**

German Coast Slave Revolt

Government under the U.S. Constitution (ratified in 1788) begins

Albany Congress

Onondaga nation head, Canasatego, speaks for the Haudenosaunee at the Treaty of Lancaster

The Library Company is founded

Tuscarora nation joins the Haudenosaunee Confederacy

1811 **1789** **1754** **1744** **1731** **1722**

Reconstruction Act of 1867

Treaty of Fort Laramie, aka Sioux Treaty of 1868, is signed

Fourteenth Amendment is ratified

American Library Association is founded

Compromise of 1877

Nineteenth Amendment is introduced to Congress

Harriet Powers creates the Bible Quilt

1867 **1868** **1876** **1877** **1878** **1886**

Triangle Shirtwaist Fire

New York Factory Investigating Commission is formed

National Association for the Advancement of Colored People (NAACP) is founded

Uprising of the 20,000 labor strike

Plessy v. Ferguson passes by a vote of 7 to 1, upholding racial segregation as constitutional

Queen Lili'uokalani creates the Queen's Quilt

Matilda Joslyn Gage publishes *Woman, Church and State*

Hull House is founded

1911 **1909** **1896** **1895** **1893** **1889**

Federal Theatre Project is created

Frances Perkins is appointed first Secretary of Labor

The Cradle Will Rock opera is performed despite government pushback

House Committee on Un-American Activities is formed

International Sweethearts of Rhythm is formed

World War II begins

Congress eliminates the Federal Theatre Project

Billie Holiday performs "Strange Fruit"

Red Scare

Japan's military strike on Pearl Harbor

US enters World War II

1933 **1937** **1938** **1939** **1940** **1941**

RAD AMERICAN HISTORY A-Z

RAD AMERICAN HISTORY A-Z

MOVEMENTS & MOMENTS THAT DEMONSTRATE THE POWER OF THE PEOPLE

WRITTEN BY
KATE SCHATZ

ILLUSTRATED BY
MIRIAM KLEIN STAHL

TEN SPEED PRESS
California | New York

CONTENTS

"History is not the past. It is the stories we tell about the past."

—GRACE LEE BOGGS, AUTHOR AND ACTIVIST

INTRODUCTION

CURB CUTS, CONSCIOUSNESS-RAISING, and constitutions. Supreme Court cases, voting rights, quilts, zines, and witches. Redwood trees and punk shows. Climate strikes and labor laws. The New Deal, the Bonus Army, and the only all-girl integrated jazz band in the US.

Librarians who fight for free speech. Athletes who take a knee. Children who march for freedom. Welcome to *Rad American History A–Z,* a book that explores several centuries of radical, powerful, and fascinating American histories.

We begin on Alcatraz Island in the San Francisco Bay, where hundreds of Native Americans occupied an abandoned prison to draw attention to the plight of their people in 1969. We end in New York City's Zuccotti Park, the tiny public space in lower Manhattan where the Occupy Wall Street movement began in 2011. In between, we range from Reconstruction to Riot Grrrl, from the East Coast to the West, and from the 16th century to the 21st.

We've selected these stories for a number of reasons. For one, we think they're *rad,* in the sense that they're just really cool. For another, they also present different perspectives on how those who are considered radical have shaped and transformed America. These are people and groups with big ideas and outrageous creativity; people who have dared to be different, to fight for their rights, to create something new, and to defy unjust laws and corrupt power. In the words of Representative Alexandria Ocasio-Cortez: "It only has ever been radicals that have changed this country."

RAD AMERICAN HISTORY A–Z is, of course, incomplete—because it's a collection of stories about history, and every single book about history is incomplete. It's impossible to include every important moment in American history, or every major significant social movement. Think of this as a sampling, a *glimpse* into just a few of the thousands of stories that have contributed to American history, and to the centuries-old movement for justice, equality, and truth.

Rad American History A–Z is also biased—toward the stories that don't get told, the ones many readers won't have heard of: stories of women, people of color, immigrants, indigenous people, and those whose histories aren't always seen as important or central to the American story. These are the stories and truths that many people would prefer to deny, the details that often get ignored, glossed over, sanitized, or left out—especially in history books.

Here are stories of police brutality, racial terrorism, discriminatory laws and policies, the repression of women, and the mass incarceration of innocent Americans. But here too are stories of triumph, resilience, resistance, creation, and hope. The history of America cannot be boiled down to one single story, told from one single perspective—it is thousands and thousands of compelling, inspiring, sometimes shocking stories, told from the points of view of the diverse humans who've populated this land. *Rad American History A–Z* explores how we got to where we are now—and what we need to know about our histories in order to create a just, sustainable future.

HISTORY IS NEVER NEUTRAL—it's never *not* political or somehow separate from culture and experience. The histories we learn are always shaped by the one doing the documenting, the teaching, the writing, the telling.

As artists, we made specific decisions on every page of this book. Some were practical: details got left out, due to word count and page limits. But beyond that, we made very intentional choices about which stories to include—and how to tell them. Where to begin and end? What points of view do we include? What might surprise, excite, and engage readers? What do we want people to know about America?

Our approach to answering these questions was to talk to people: to scholars and historians and journalists and movement leaders. To college professors and high school and middle school history teachers. And also: to the people who were *there*. The people who have participated in the moments and movements we explore, and those who are descended from the folks who once did. These generous and wise individuals shared their insight, their experiences, and their expertise, and helped us shape each story, and the book as a whole.

We asked them: What stories are you excited to see included? What is *not* there? Who and what are we overlooking? We reached out to people about specific stories and asked: What's a little-known aspect of this history that we might explore? What do people often get wrong about this event or movement—and how does your community want this story to be told?

LANADA WAR JACK, the first Native American woman to attend UC Berkeley, described what it was like to arrive on Alcatraz Island that night in 1969. Leroy Hill, a speaker for the Grand Council of the Haudenosaunee (Iroquois) Confederacy, clarified the political and cultural history of his people.

Eric Reiss shared stories about his late mother, Dr. Louise Reiss, whose pioneering work on the effects of nuclear radiation has long gone unrecognized. Tony Uranday, the son of the late farmworker and organizer Esther Uranday, also offered memories of growing up with a remarkable mother.

Judy Nagosian and Joan Ditzion talked about what it was like to write *Our Bodies, Ourselves,* the bestselling women's health book of all time. Barbara Smith explained specific details about the early days of the Combahee River Collective. Alicia Garza discussed how she feels about being called the "founder" of Black Lives Matter.

Musician Corin Tucker and artist Tammy Rae Carland shared memories of their first encounters with Riot Grrrl. Amanda Yates Garcia described the witchcraft lineage she's descended from. David Solnit offered anecdotes from the antinuclear protests he attended in Nevada in the 1980s. And multiple young climate activists detailed what they're doing to protect the planet—and why it matters so much.

This process was especially important because of our own limited experiences and perspectives as white women creating a book like this. While we strive to be antiracist, and to share histories in the most respectful, accurate ways, we were brought up in educational and cultural systems that placed white people—mostly men—at the center of history and failed to teach us so much. Part of writing a book like this is unlearning our own internalized white supremacy, and we're grateful to those who have offered corrections and pointed to places where we've needed to deepen our research and do better.

WE ALSO DREW UPON our own experiences and memories—these are valid forms of history-telling too. We toured a Center for Independent Living; we explored the extensive archives of Sister Corita Kent with the archivists who preserve her work. Miriam remembered her days as a young punk attending Riot Grrrl shows; Kate looked back at photos from Earth First! demonstrations she attended at Headwaters Forest in the 1990s; and we both recalled moments from the Occupy movement.

Miriam's great-aunt Doris worked at the Triangle Shirtwaist Factory. She wasn't there on the day of the deadly fire, but she's there in the illustration that Miriam created. And the X chapter (pages 148–149) is inspired by our own high school history notebooks. It represents both the histories we *wish* we'd been taught, as well as the histories we have taught ourselves in the years since, as teachers, as activists, as history geeks, and

as feminists looking to the past in order to understand our future.

We learned *a lot* while making this book, and we hope that you'll also learn a few new things—about your history, your culture, your country, and yourself.

Thanks for reading, and for being *rad.*

Love,
Kate & Miriam

"If to believe in freedom and equality is to be a radical, then I am a radical."
—REPRESENTATIVE PATSY MINK, FIRST WOMAN OF COLOR ELECTED TO CONGRESS

A

IS FOR
ALCATRAZ

AND THE INDIAN OCCUPATION OF 1969

"We hold the Rock!"
—FROM THE ALCATRAZ PROCLAMATION

IT WAS 2:00 A.M. on a chilly November night when the first boats set sail for the rocky island in the middle of San Francisco Bay. Alcatraz, the site of the infamous federal prison that once housed gangster Al Capone, had been abandoned and unused for years. The people on board the boats huddled together with their sleeping bags and backpacks, hearts racing as they made the crossing.

The 79 women and men on the boat had several things in common: they were all college students, they were all activists, and, though they came from different tribes, they were all

Native American. And they were planning to take over Alcatraz, also known as "The Rock," to protest centuries of injustices committed against their people.

Would the Coast Guard stop them, or would they make it onto Alcatraz? Would their plan actually work? And if they did make it, what would happen next?

THE LATE 1960S WERE a time of tremendous social, political, and cultural transformation all across America, but especially in the San Francisco Bay Area. Radical change was everywhere you looked—from the Black Panthers serving free breakfast to children in West Oakland to free-speech rallies and anti-Vietnam war demonstrations in Berkeley to long-haired hippies and the Summer of Love in the Haight-Ashbury neighborhood of San Francisco.

Colleges and universities were major sites of organizing, as more and more students became politically active and began to question war, inequality, and cultural conformity. Ethnic groups who'd long been marginalized from mainstream American life were coming together to denounce racism and demand recognition and equality—and the Indian students heading out to Alcatraz had been a big part of that.

Many of them had met through the Third World Liberation Front (TWLF), a coalition of Black, Latino, Asian, and Native American student groups at California colleges that spoke out against the lack of diversity on campuses and in curriculum. TWLF held a months-long strike in 1968 and 1969 that led to the creation of the first Ethnic Studies department in the country—and that empowered the Indian students, who were part of the first generation of Native

Americans to attend college, to continue their activism.

THE BOATS MADE IT to Alcatraz, where the lighthouse emitted a steady beam, and the cellblocks towered above, empty and dark. The new Alcatraz residents saw the twinkling lights of San Francisco, Oakland, and Berkeley across the bay. They saw Coast Guard ships headed their way, with powerful searchlights sweeping the dark waters. They found their way to the empty cells and unrolled their sleeping bags to get some rest—but not before they celebrated by drumming and singing songs.

They didn't know what the morning would bring, but these committed organizers believed in what they were doing. They didn't know that more boats full of Native people would come in the days to follow. They didn't know they'd end up on the front page of the newspaper; that hundreds would soon join them for a massive Thanksgiving feast and pow wow honoring the *real* stories of their ancestors. And they had no idea that the occupation would last 19 months, capture the attention of the entire nation, and lead to historic legislative and cultural change.

THE HISTORY OF INDIGENOUS Native American residents and European immigrants spans several centuries of struggle, heartbreak, resilience, and survival. From the earliest days of the Europeans' arrival in the "New World," indigenous North Americans have fought to retain their land, their cultures and customs, and their lives. In the effort to claim as much land as possible, white Americans used violence and war, as well as legal tactics like treaties and federal policies. During the 18th, 19th, and 20th centuries, almost 400 treaties were ratified between the American government and Native American tribes. Nearly all of them have been broken, violated, or changed by the government to suit its own needs.

The 19th-century government policies of Manifest Destiny and westward expansion saw Native people forced off their ancestral lands and placed onto reservations. During the later part of the 19th century, a series of off-reservation boarding schools were set up in order to "civilize" Indian children and teach them the "proper" ways of white people. Native children were taken from their families, often by force, and made to cut their hair, dress in "proper" clothes, convert to Christianity, and speak English only. These policies devastated Indian families, many of whom resisted the removal of their children, and were punished by police.

To manage all the land it was taking, the government created the Bureau of Indian Affairs in 1824. By 1950, the bureau was led by the same man who oversaw the incarceration of Japanese American citizens during World War II (see page 65). He announced a new policy of "termination" to break up the reservation system, disband tribes, sell Indian land, and relocate Indians to urban areas so they could assimilate by losing their distinct identities and becoming like "normal Americans"—aka white Americans.

More than 11,000 Native people and their families moved from rural lands to cities like Oakland, San Francisco, and Los Angeles. But Indians arriving in these new cities found very little support. By the mid-1960s, more than 40,000 Indians from nearly 100 tribal groups lived in the San Francisco Bay Area, with the majority working low-paying jobs and facing discrimination and police brutality. They struggled to access decent schools and affordable, safe housing. It was hard to feel a sense of community, and tribal identity was nearly impossible to maintain.

IT WAS THIS LENGTHY history of trauma and loss that the Alcatraz occupiers brought with them: many of them were the children and grandchildren of Indians who'd been forcibly assimilated, and they were ready to be the generation that reclaimed Indian identity and land.

They released a public proclamation that began "We, the Native Americans, reclaim the land known as Alcatraz Island in the name of all American Indians." They cited an 1868 treaty the United States had signed with the Sioux tribe, exerting their right to claim unused federal land. Alcatraz Prison was closed in 1963, making the island exactly that. The group laid out a vision: they wanted to build a Center for Native American Studies, an American Indian Spiritual Center, an Indian Center of Ecology, an arts and crafts center, and a restaurant serving traditional Indian foods. One of the lead occupiers, LaNada War Jack, worked with a local architecture firm to build a scale model of it all.

Within days of the occupation, the abandoned buildings and desolate landscape were transformed. Signs that had read UNITED STATES PROPERTY soon proclaimed UNITED INDIAN PROPERTY, and the words INDIAN LAND were spray-painted all over the island. Tipis were built, and strategy meetings were held inside them. A small team of women and men took on leadership roles and spent their days communicating with journalists, negotiating with politicians, and debating the best strategies to get their important messages out to the world.

Everyone pitched in and took on a job: there was food prep, security detail, sanitation crew, and more. A nurse opened a health clinic, and three women started a childcare center and school, where parents volunteered to teach traditional school subjects as well as Native American history. The children learned some of the games, songs, and art that government boarding schools had once tried to erase.

BACK ON THE MAINLAND, federal and city officials grappled with how to deal with the occupation. At first they wanted to send the Coast Guard to force everyone off the island. But the occupation had overwhelming public support: polls showed that most people believed the government should give Alcatraz to the Indians. So the officials decided to wait it out, assuming the occupiers would eventually give up. In the meantime, money, food, clothing, and supplies poured in from supporters all over the country.

Over the next 19 months, more than 5,000 people came to Alcatraz. Many came just for a day, to see what it was all about—journalists and artists, sightseers and hippies, families with children, and curious college students. But most of those who came were Indians of all ages, many of whom traveled long distances to get there: college students from Oregon and Southern California; elders from reservations in Kansas, Arizona, and New Mexico; even indigenous people from Mexico and Canada. Though these Indians all had distinct customs, languages, and identities, they still felt a common bond.

Every evening they came together around blazing campfires to dance, tell stories, and share laughter and memories. The occupiers of Alcatraz weren't there only to make a political statement; they were also creating a community. While some had lived on reservations their entire lives, others had been young children when their families relocated from tribal land to cities. For many, it was their first experience spending time around other Indians outside of their immediate family. A sense of "Indianness" was celebrated, especially among those who'd grown up feeling ashamed, or completely unaware, of their heritage.

The occupiers published a nationally distributed newsletter, and broadcast *Radio Free Alcatraz*, ensuring that the story of Alcatraz was being told by those who were there, in addition to the national media coverage. Grace Thorpe, daughter of Olympic medalist and football star Jim Thorpe, coordinated publicity, and was able to get donations of money and much-needed supplies while spreading the word about the occupiers' efforts. People across the country—including the president—were finally paying attention to the voices and struggles of Indians.

IN JULY 1970, just over seven months into the Alcatraz occupation, President Richard Nixon announced an end to the "termination policy," declaring it "ineffective and demeaning." Back on Alcatraz, this was seen as a victory—but organizers knew the fight was far from over. The leadership council continued to negotiate with the government, who wanted the occupiers off the island immediately but didn't want to risk public outrage by forcibly removing them. The council knew that staying on the island was the only way to have enough leverage to get the rest of their demands met.

But life on Alcatraz wasn't easy, and the occupation began to struggle. Many of the students had to leave and resume school, and some found the living conditions too harsh, especially during the cold, rainy winter. Some felt that the occupiers had already made their point, or that the leaders lacked a long-term strategy; others were unhappy with the waves of new people who'd come to stay on the island and didn't always share the peaceful vision of the original occupiers.

By the end of May 1971, the government had cut off all utility service to the island; the public responded by donating generators and barrels of fresh water. On June 11, 1971, 19 months after the first boats arrived, the occupation of Alcatraz came to an end when three Coast Guard vessels and a helicopter arrived, filled with armed FBI agents. The final 15 occupiers left peacefully, without the deed to the land.

BUT THE IMPACT OF the Alcatraz occupation went far beyond the physical presence of people on the island. It transformed public perception of urban Indians, strengthened the American Indian movement, and helped shape federal Indian policy for decades. In the wake of the occupation, Congress passed several major pieces of legislation, including the Indian Self-Determination and Education Act and the Indian Health Care Act. Sacred land was returned to tribes in New Mexico, Alaska, and Washington. And many of the occupiers became leaders within Native American communities as professors, scholars, activists, filmmakers, and tribal leaders. Grace Thorpe worked closely with members of Congress to advocate for Native American communities. Wilma Mankiller, a struggling young mother when she came to Alcatraz, was inspired to return to her tribal land, where she became the first woman elected as Chief of the Cherokee Nation and one of America's most important 20th-century Native American leaders.

As scholar Dr. LaNada War Jack says, "The victories were hard to see at the time, but they came into fruition later on. . . . It was the reidentification. We reclaimed our identity. It was OK to be Native, we no longer had to be ashamed. And once you identity as Native, you want to know more about your tribe, your culture, your language, your ceremony, your songs."

On Alcatraz, and in the years that followed, a spirit of Native pride, identity, and resistance was reborn.

A IS ALSO FOR . . .

ABOLITIONISM: The movement to abolish slavery.

ACT-UP (THE AIDS COALITION TO UNLEASH POWER): An activist group formed in 1987 committed to improving the lives of people living with HIV and AIDS through radical public demonstrations.

ALPHA SUFFRAGE CLUB: An African American women's suffrage club started by Ida B. Wells-Barnett in Chicago in 1913.

ATTICA PRISON UPRISING: A prison rebellion in New York State in 1971, when 1,281 inmates at Attica Correctional Facility rose up to demand better living conditions.

B

IS FOR
#BLACKLIVES MATTER

THE MOVEMENT THAT STARTED WITH THREE FRIENDS AND THREE WORDS

"Every successful social movement in this country's history has used disruption as a key strategy to fight for social change."
—ALICIA GARZA, COFOUNDER OF #BLACKLIVESMATTER

LIKE MANY AMERICANS, Alicia Garza spent July 13, 2013, anxiously waiting to hear the verdict in a high-profile criminal case. A man named George Zimmerman was on trial for shooting and killing Trayvon Martin, a 17-year-old he saw walking through his Sanford, Florida, neighborhood one evening. George thought Trayvon, who was African American, looked suspicious. He thought he might be a burglar. But Trayvon was just a teenager walking home from a convenience store, where he'd bought Skittles and an iced tea. George called the police, but before they arrived, he shot Trayvon in the chest. There were no witnesses.

Trayvon's death set off a huge public outcry. George said he had acted in self-defense, claiming that Trayvon had attacked him. At first the police didn't plan to file charges, but after extensive media coverage, combined with the outrage of community members and activists, they charged George with second-degree murder. The trial was followed closely around the country, with many holding out hope that prosecuting this act of violence against an innocent young man would lead to justice for Trayvon's family.

THE JURY DELIBERATED FOR 16 hours. Alicia and her friends sat at a bar in Oakland, California, checking their phones for updates on the verdict. Finally, it was there on her Facebook feed: *NOT GUILTY.* Alicia felt like she'd been punched in the gut. She was enraged—but she wasn't surprised. Statistics show that unarmed black Americans are far more likely than white Americans to be stopped by police, suspected of a crime, arrested, convicted, and imprisoned. As a black woman and activist, Alicia knew the statistics—and the realities—very well. Many people in her community struggled with police brutality and harassment.

She knew the truth about racial profiling, how people who look like Trayvon are more likely to be seen as suspicious. She knew that when white civilians shoot black and brown people, the incidents are eight times more likely to be declared "justified" by juries and judges. And she knew that police officers are rarely, if ever, punished for killing innocent people, especially black and brown ones. But even with that knowledge, she had still hoped that this time would be different.

Alicia thought about her own brother, who was around the same age and height as Trayvon. Would he be seen as threatening, even though he'd never been in a fight? Would he be next? What would it take to make other people care as much as she did?

To Alicia Garza, on that summer evening, it felt like the lives of people who looked like her, her brother, her friends, and those in her neighborhood, *just didn't matter.*

TO EXPRESS HER GRIEF, Alicia turned to Facebook, where she wrote a long, emotional post: "I continue to be surprised at how little black lives matter." She ended with "Black people. I love you. I love us. Our lives matter." Her post gained a rapidly growing number of likes and shares.

One person who saw truth in Alicia's post was her friend Patrisse Cullors. Patrisse had grown up in Los Angeles, in a neighborhood where tensions with police ran high. She was just a child when she watched her brothers, who were simply playing outside, be searched and thrown against a wall by officers. She saw how the police treated people from her community differently from the people in the wealthy white community where she went to school. She often asked herself: *Why is it like this?*

Patrisse was in a motel room about 300 miles north of Oakland that night, but reading Alicia's post made her feel connected. She shared the post on her own page, and she added a hashtag: *#BlackLivesMatter.*

It was a simple yet powerful phrase. #BlackLivesMatter occurred to Patrisse as an echo of Alicia's sentiment: that the lives of black Americans *don't* seem to matter to the police, to juries and judges, to politicians, and to most white Americans. And as Patrisse saw more emotional posts from friends, she wanted to make them feel loved, heard, and seen. She shared the hashtag. She tweeted it out. #BlackLivesMatter, she wrote, over and over that night.

The next day, Patrisse posted on Alicia's Facebook wall: "#blacklivesmatter campaign? can we discuss this? i have ideas." This post caught the eye of another black woman activist: Opal Tometi. Opal, the daughter of Nigerian immigrants, was working in New York for an immigrant rights organization. She had experience using social media for political campaigns; she reached out to Alicia and Patrisse, and they got to work.

They created Tumblr and Twitter accounts, asking people to share their own stories about why black lives matter. In downtown Oakland, a local shoe store let Alicia and another activist paint the words in huge block letters on their windows. In Los Angeles, Patrisse led a march with the words printed on a large banner. And over the next year, the hashtag spread across social media, popping up regularly on Facebook, Twitter, and Tumblr.

IF THE #BLACKLIVESMATTER movement began that July, it fully emerged one year later, after another tragic police shooting of an unarmed black man. On August 9, 2014, 18-year-old Michael Brown was shot in the back by a police officer in Ferguson, Missouri, just outside St. Louis. The area had a long history of tension between the majority-black residents and the majority-white police force and city government. In the wake of the shooting, community members began to gather: some at peaceful vigils, and others in emotional protests that sometimes resulted in property damage and violence.

The city cracked down hard on the demonstrations, imposing curfews and sending in police with military-style equipment. The activity caught the attention of the media and the public, and soon #BlackLivesMatter (BLM) was trending like never before. The BLM founders decided to transform their virtual impact into on-the-ground support for the Ferguson community. They connected with other organizers to set up "freedom rides" to get activists from across the country to Ferguson, inspired by the freedom rides of the civil rights movement, when hundreds of black and white activists rode public buses together to protest segregation. Soon hundreds of people were headed to Ferguson to help support the local community.

When Alicia, Patrisse, and Opal arrived in Ferguson, they were stunned to see #BlackLivesMatter everywhere. Those three words that Patrisse had typed out were now printed on giant banners and written with Sharpies on handmade cardboard signs. They were chanted in the streets by people they'd never met, in a city they'd never been to. As an experienced organizer, Alicia knew that social change usually takes a long time, and that many people don't get to see the transformations they fight for. But in that moment, in Ferguson, she could tell: this was different.

The women were faced with a decision: how do you turn a social media moment into a real movement? Tweets and posts wouldn't save black lives. They needed to act fast, but they also wanted to be strategic. Although Alicia, Patrisse, and Opal were the ones who got the BLM organization going, they didn't want to be *in charge*; they wanted to empower black leaders to build movements in their own communities. They trained local activists in Ferguson, and encouraged those who'd come to Ferguson from other cities to start their own BLM chapters back home.

SADLY, MICHAEL BROWN WAS not the only innocent black person killed by police in 2014. #BlackLivesMatter activists organized in response to the shootings of Eric Garner in New York City, Akai Gurley in Los Angeles, Laquan McDonald in Chicago, and 12-year old Tamir Rice, killed at a playground in Cleveland, Ohio, in November. That same month, when a grand jury decided not to charge the officer who killed Michael Brown, "Black lives matter!" chants were heard across the nation. Protests erupted from New York City to Ferguson to Oakland.

While this racial unrest, protest, and violence was nothing new, what *was* new was the impact of technology. A social media post could result in a mass protest. A cellphone video could capture an arrest, a shooting, or a police confrontation—making something that had historically been invisible not just visible, but *viral*. The combination of social media *and* a recognizable movement like #BlackLivesMatter brought the issues of police brutality and racial injustice to the forefront of national conversations.

#BlackLivesMatter also began to show up in popular culture. The phrase was uttered by tennis champion Serena Williams and President Barack Obama. It was mentioned on TV shows, and it appeared on T-shirts and hoodies, mugs and bumper stickers.

Suddenly it seemed to be everywhere—and with that came a backlash. The BLM founders and members have received death threats, harassment, and constant criticism. They have been called racists, cop-haters, terrorists—and worse.

Some nonblack people feel threatened or left out by the phrase "Black lives matter." What about us? they've argued. Why single out *black* lives? Don't *all* lives matter? The answer is: Yes, of course every human life matters. But until all humans are actually treated equally in this country, it is justified—and vital—to bring attention to certain groups who have been routinely, statistically, and historically harmed.

When young people learn about the civil rights movement, they tend to learn about great men like Dr. Martin Luther King Jr., Representative John Lewis, and Malcolm X. Aside from Rosa Parks, it's rare to learn about the *women* who drove the movement, like Diane Nash, Dorothy Height, and Jo Ann Robinson. Alicia, Opal, and Patrisse have experienced some of this: high-profile articles about BLM have failed to mention their names, and more than one magazine has featured male BLM activists on glossy covers, leaving the women out of the picture.

While they do want credit for their efforts, Alicia always points out that they didn't *found* the fight for racial justice, or even start something brand-new. Movements happen over long periods of time, and BLM is one point on a long trajectory of organizing for racial justice. "We created an organization," Alicia explains, "that gave people space to reimagine what's possible by insisting that black lives matter."

B IS ALSO FOR . . .

BEAT GENERATION: A literary movement that emerged from San Francisco in the 1950s, reflecting the postwar counterculture in poetry, novels, and plays.

BIRTH CONTROL PILL: The first oral contraceptive pill for women, widely available by 1960.

BLACK PANTHER PARTY: A black political organization founded in Oakland, California, in 1966 by Huey Newton and Bobby Seale.

BROWN BERETS: A social justice organization committed to the civil rights of the Latinx community founded in the mid-1960s.

BROWN V. BOARD OF EDUCATION: The 1954 Supreme Court case that declared segregation in schools unconstitutional.

COLIN TAKES A KNEE

DURING A PRESEASON FOOTBALL game in August 2016, San Francisco 49ers backup quarterback Colin Kaepernick made a decision that would change the course of his career. While his teammates all stood for the national anthem, Colin stayed seated. He did it again during the next game.

At first, no one really noticed. When a journalist asked him about it after the third game, he explained: "I am not going to stand up to show pride in a flag for a country that oppresses black people and people of color."

Colin, born to a white mother and black father, was reacting to recent unrest across America: protests in Ferguson, Missouri; the rise of the #BlackLivesMatter movement; and the back-to-back police shootings of two unarmed black men, Alton Sterling and Philando Castile. He was angry and frustrated, and he decided it was time to take a stand—by *not* standing.

Some argued that Colin was being disrespectful and unpatriotic; others appreciated him for bringing attention to important matters, pointing out that racist policies in America were *more* disrespectful than his actions.

Colin remained firm in his beliefs, but he was also willing to listen: based on feedback from members of the military, he began kneeling, instead of sitting.

On opening week of the regular season, millions of viewers tuned in. They saw Colin take a knee—but he wasn't alone. One of his teammates knelt with him. Four other players raised their fists in the air. Throughout the week, other players knelt and raised fists as well, including soccer player Megan Rapinoe.

The raised fists recalled one of the most famous sports protests of all time: when, while standing on the medal podium at the 1968 Olympics in Mexico City, American track stars Tommie Smith and John Carlos took off their shoes, unzipped their jackets, and raised their black-gloved fists in the Black Power salute in protest of racial injustice.

In some ways, these acts all seem simple. But quiet protests can speak volumes—and they take immense courage. Colin's decision in particular became a huge story; his actions, combined with the coverage of #BlackLivesMatter, led to difficult but necessary conversations about racism and the realities of police violence.

Many also believe that it caused him to lose his football career: after a season of quiet protests and intense media coverage, Colin became a free agent, and no NFL team would sign him. The teams all said it was because he wasn't as good as he once was, but Colin believed otherwise. He'd always known the risk he was taking. "If they take football away," he told a reporter, "I know that I stood up for what is right."

C

IS FOR

COMBAHEE RIVER RAID

AND ONE WOMAN'S ROLE IN THE BATTLE THAT LIBERATED HUNDREDS OF PEOPLE

ON JUNE 1, 1863, two boats made their way, slow and steady, up South Carolina's Combahee River, a short, twisting waterway, one of the many tidal rivers that reaches inland from the Atlantic Ocean, snaking through South Carolina's low country. Along its rich, fertile banks at that time were valuable rice fields, some of the wealthiest plantations in the state, and hundreds, maybe even thousands, of enslaved men, women, and children.

This was deep in Confederate territory, and these were Union boats under the command of Colonel James Montgomery. On board were 300 Union soldiers, almost of all them free black men who'd signed up to help fight in the American Civil War. It was nighttime and pitch black; there was no moon.

The soldiers moved up the river, planning to take the plantation owners—and Confederate troops—by surprise. The Union's attack would provide cover for the enslaved people to escape; they'd run down to the river and board the boats. That was the plan: destroy the plantations, confiscate goods, and liberate as many people as possible.

At the helm of the lead vessel, a steamboat named the *John Adams*, were three Union spies. Charles Simmons and Samuel Hayward were skilled navigators—former slaves who knew the river well. They had escaped, and now they were helping to lead a raid unlike any other. The third spy on board was the woman who had recruited them to join the military effort. She'd been laying the groundwork for this raid for months, gathering intelligence and acting as the crucial link between the military generals and the black community, whether still enslaved or recently escaped.

She had assembled a 10-man team of spies, including Charles and Samuel, and sent word to the enslaved people on the plantations to let them know liberation was coming. She worked to gain the trust of freed men, paying them to give her strategic information, such as how many people lived on each plantation, and where to stop along the river so they could rescue the most folks at a time. Her name was Harriet Tubman.

HARRIET TUBMAN WAS BORN Araminta Ross sometime between 1820 and 1822. She took the name Harriet Tubman when she was in her twenties, but she was also known by other names. Her childhood nickname was "Minty," and the abolitionist John Brown referred to her as "General." To the hundreds of people she helped get to freedom, she was known as "Moses," after the biblical figure who helped the enslaved Israelites escape Egypt.

Many people think that Harriet Tubman founded the Underground Railroad, the vast, secretive network of homes, churches, and anti-slavery allies that guided thousands of people to freedom during the 19th century. In fact, the Underground Railroad came into existence before Harriet was even born. But Harriet was one of the railroad's most legendary and successful "conductors," the term used for those who guided the escapees out of slavery and along the stations of the network. It's estimated that Harriet made nearly 20 trips to the South and led more than 300 people to free states and Canada—including her brothers and her elderly parents, whom she rescued on her final mission. And before she was a conductor, Harriet used stations on the Underground Railroad to escape to freedom herself, in 1849.

IN 1861, CONFEDERATE TROOPS fired on Fort Sumter, and the American Civil War began. Harriet was well known within abolitionist circles by then; like many other Northerners, she rushed to support the Union's effort. In 1862 she traveled south to Port Royal, an island right off the coast of South Carolina where the Union had established a kind of refugee camp for newly freed black men, women, and children.

At first, Harriet worked as a nurse, tending to battle wounds and treating patients with contagious diseases like typhoid, dysentery, and smallpox. She used her knowledge of natural herbal remedies to treat them; the fact that she never got sick herself led many to believe that she had supernatural powers. At night, after long days working in the hospital and community, she made root beer, gingerbread, and pies to sell to the soldiers for a little money.

On January 1, 1863, President Abraham Lincoln issued the Emancipation Proclamation, legally freeing all enslaved people in Southern states—in theory. While it was an important step toward the abolition of slavery, the Emancipation Proclamation didn't automatically free all enslaved people. Because the Confederate states were still in rebellion, they didn't recognize Lincoln as president, and in many cases, continued to follow their own laws, including the chattel slavery system.

The proclamation was significant, though, because it put the question of slavery at the center of the war. It also allowed black men to join the Union army, and many newly freed men were able to join the fight. But, despite President Lincoln's infamous proclamation, hundreds of thousands of people remained enslaved, unable to leave the plantation prisons.

A KANSAS COLONEL NAMED John Montgomery arrived at Port Royal in February of 1863. He had fought alongside John Brown, the radical abolitionist who believed in using violence to end slavery. Colonel Montgomery had heard all about the legendary Harriet Tubman: he knew of her bravery, her navigational skills, and her ability to communicate with and gain the trust of frightened and traumatized communities. Harriet knew that Colonel Montgomery was one of John Brown's trusted men. So when Montgomery and several other anti-slavery Union officers approached her to help plan a raid to free enslaved people in the region, she agreed. And when it came time to finally embark on the Combahee River raid, Harriet was right there at Colonel Montgomery's side.

THE COMBAHEE IS SHALLOW, its bottom muddy, and its banks wide and marshy. Thanks to Harriet's scouting missions, the boats managed to avoid the hidden mines and torpedoes that floated just beneath the water's surface. Around dawn they made their first stop, and a small troop of men slipped into the marshes to make their way inland. As expected, the Confederate troops were caught off guard. But they managed to send a messenger up the river, to spread the warning.

The Union troops got to work. They raided the stores, warehouses, and outbuildings, confiscating armloads of valuable commodities and livestock, and foods like rice, potatoes, and corn. Whatever they couldn't carry, they burned—including the rice fields, the mansions, and the surrounding buildings. Many of the Union soldiers were formerly enslaved; some even destroyed the very plantations where they had been forced to live and work, liberating their friends, families, and former communities. Black smoke rose up from each burning structure.

Word spread fast to hundreds of enslaved men, women, and children: the raid is here. It's happening. *Freedom*. They rushed down from the fields to the riverbank, carrying babies, personal items, valuable animals. Harriet stayed with the boats, helping people onboard, singing songs, and calling to the crowds along the shore.

At each stop, the Union troops rushed in, and the enslaved people rushed out, filling the boats. At one point, Harriet saw a woman struggling to carry her baby and two pigs. As she took the pigs in her arms and helped the woman onboard, Harriet tripped on the hem of her long dress, tearing it to shreds. A few weeks later, she wrote a letter to abolitionist friends up north, asking them to please send her some "bloomers," the name for the brand-new style of women's pants. Harriet wrote that she would never again wear a dress on an expedition—pants only!

The boats headed back down the river, packed with newly freed people and their victorious rescuers. The raid was an overwhelming success. Military reports indicated that more than 700 enslaved people were liberated on that single day, with only one non-Confederate life lost. The estates of nine of the most prestigious slave-holding families in the state were destroyed, and Union troops made off with thousands of dollars in goods. The raid economically crippled one of the richest regions in the South and showed that black soldiers could be successful in strategy and in battle.

THE COMBAHEE RIVER RAID was the largest liberation of enslaved people in American history. And while Harriet herself didn't fight or even officially lead the operation, none of it would have been possible without her.

When Colonel Montgomery submitted his official military report after the Combahee River raid, he didn't mention Harriet—not because she was unimportant, but because he didn't want to put her in danger by making her identity public. Harriet's ability to operate in secret was one of the keys to her success, both as a conductor and as a Union spy.

That all changed a month later, when a Boston newspaper ran a front-page article celebrating the raid, and declaring that "The whole venture owed its success to the complete preliminary survey made by Harriet Tubman's espionage troops."

Harriet's work as a spy was no longer a secret, but she continued to work for the Union as a scout and nurse until the Confederate surrender in 1865. She wasn't paid for her efforts because she wasn't an official member of the military. She applied for a pension, describing her roles as "nurse, spy and cook," but she didn't receive any money until 1899—nearly 35 years later.

Harriet lived to the age of 93, and her legacy has endured: she is one of the most famous black Americans of the 19th century, but the full story of her work hasn't always been acknowledged or understood.

C IS ALSO FOR . . .

CHESAPEAKE, OHIO & SOUTHWESTERN RAILROAD COMPANY V. IDA B. WELLS: An 1885 court case filed against the state of Tennessee by 20-year-old Ida B. Wells, a black woman who was forcibly removed from a train car, despite having a paid ticket.

CHICAGO DEFENDER: A highly influential and widely read weekly newspaper for the black community, founded in 1905 by journalist Robert S. Abbott.

CHINESE EXCLUSION ACT: The 1882 US federal law that prohibited the immigration of Chinese laborers, and the first federal law to prevent members of a specific ethnic group from immigrating.

CRITICAL RESISTANCE: A national grassroots organization founded in 1997 that works to dismantle the prison-industrial complex.

COMBAHEE RIVER COLLECTIVE

IN 1974, A CENTURY after Harriet Tubman's successful Civil War raid, a group of black feminist activists came together to organize the Boston chapter of the National Black Feminist Organization (NBFO). By 1975 the group had decided to become an independent organization, calling themselves the Combahee River Collective. Their manifesto, "The Combahee River Collective Statement," is a landmark 20th-century feminist text.

The members of the Combahee Collective were part of the feminist movement, and had been active in other progressive movements of the late 1960s. They were committed to justice and liberation for all people, but they shared a growing frustration that the lives and needs of black women, and lesbians in particular, were not being considered. The group, which included women like Sharon Bourke, Demita Frazier, Eleanor Johnson, Margo Okazawa-Rey, and twin sisters Barbara Smith and Beverly Smith, began as a way for them to explore the ramifications of black women's multiple oppressions and to do innovative organizing to increase black women's freedom.

Barbara Smith had read a biography about Harriet Tubman that mentioned her role in the Combahee River raid. She suggested using the name for the group as a way to honor Harriet, and to draw attention to a little-known aspect of black women's history.

The Combahee River Collective met for several years and in 1977 they wrote the Combahee River Collective Statement. Published two years later, in 1979, the Statement explores and explains the ways that issues of race, gender, sexuality, and class are all connected (what we now know as "intersectionality") and specifically discusses the political situation of black lesbian women.

It addresses the fact that black women, women of color, and working women "have been involved in the feminist movement from its start, but both outside reactionary forces and racism and elitism within the movement itself have served to obscure our participation." It names many key black feminist ancestors, including Sojourner Truth, Frances E. W. Harper, Mary Church Terrell, and Ida B. Wells-Barnett. It is an essential document of black feminist history.

The Statement acknowledges that social identities—your race, gender identity, sexuality, and so on—are powerful and important places from which to develop political analysis and actions. The authors are credited with the concept of *identity politics*—the idea that intersecting identities have significant impact upon your political status and your priorities for organizing.

Our Roll of Honor

Containing all the

Signatures to the "Declaration of Sentiments"

Set forth by the first

Woman's Rights Convention,

held at
Seneca Falls, New York
July 19·20, 1848

LADIES:

Lucretia Mott
Harriet Cady Eaton
Margaret Pryor
Elizabeth Ca
Eunice New
Mary Ann
Margaret
Martha C
Jane C.
Amy Po
Catheri
Mary A
Lydia
Delia Ma
Catherine
Elizabeth
Malvina S
PhebeMoshe
Catherine Sh
Deborah Scott
Sarah Hallowell
Mary M'Clintock
Mary Gilbert

Sophronia Taylor
Cynthia Davis
Plant

Rachel D. Bonnel
Betsey Tewksbury
Rhoda Palmer
Margaret Jenkins
Cynthia Fuller
Mary Martin
P. A. Culvert
Susan R. Doty
Rebecca Race
Sarah A. Mosher
Mary E. Vail
Lucy Spalding
Lovina Latham
Sarah Smith
Eliza Martin
Maria E. Wilbur
Elizabeth D. Smith
Caroline Barker
Ann Porter
Experience Gibbs
Antoinette E. Segur
Hannah J. Latham
Sarah Sisson

Richard P. Hunt
Samual D. Till
Justin Willia
Elisha Foote
Frederick
Henry
Davi

Nathan J. Milliken
S. E. Woodworth
Edward F. Underhill
George W. Pryor
Joel Bunker
IsaaC VanTassel
Thomas Dell
W. Capron
Shear

D

IS FOR

DECLARATION OF SENTIMENTS

THE DOCUMENT THAT HELPED SPARK THE WOMEN'S RIGHTS MOVEMENT

IN A SCENE FROM the hit 2015 musical *Hamilton*, the character Angelica Schuyler talks politics while flirting with Alexander Hamilton. She's been reading *Common Sense* by Thomas Paine (the pamphlet that encouraged the 13 colonies to seek independence from Great Britain), and she calls out the Declaration of Independence and its famous opening line, which declares that "all men are created equal"—but fails to mention *women*. A little more than 70 years after the Declaration of Independence was ratified, another declaration would challenge this omission.

AT THE WORLD ANTI-SLAVERY Convention, held in London in 1840, two American women met for the first time. Lucretia Mott, a well-known Quaker abolitionist, was one of the first white women in America to publicly call for the immediate end of slavery. She'd been selected as a delegate to the convention, a gathering of leaders from all over the world who were committed to abolishing slavery. Elizabeth Cady Stanton was honeymooning in Europe with her new husband; they were also active in the abolitionist movement and had decided to attend the convention.

But the all-male British convention leaders, who claimed to be committed to "universal liberty," were not exactly excited about American women attending the event, no matter how committed these women might be to the cause. The men felt it was inappropriate for women to speak in public or to be in positions of leadership. The entire first day of the convention was spent debating whether to allow American women to participate. Their final decision? The women could attend, but had to sit in a separate section. They could watch, but they could not speak.

Lucretia was angry, but she was no stranger to exclusion; she and a number of free black women, including Charlotte Forten and her daughters, had founded the Philadelphia Female Anti-Slavery Society because the American Anti-Slavery Society did not allow women. Elizabeth, who was younger and hadn't experienced as much of this sort of predjudice, was outraged. How could men claim to believe in freedom if they weren't going to respect women? In her memoir, Elizabeth recalls that she and Lucretia walked together after the convention and decided they should have their *own* convention, back home in America, to discuss the status and rights of women. Eight years later, this idea became a reality.

IN THE YEARS FOLLOWING the London convention, Lucretia had continued her role as a leader in the anti-slavery movement, while Elizabeth had moved from her bustling Boston neighborhood to a more isolated home in Seneca Falls, New York. Her husband, Henry, traveled a lot, and she grew lonely and frustrated with her limited domestic life. When Jane Hunt, a local Quaker abolitionist, heard that Lucretia Mott was coming to town, she invited Elizabeth and several other women to join Lucretia for tea. The five guests included Lucretia's sister, Martha Coffin Wright, and Mary Ann McClintock, an abolitionist whose house was a stop on the Underground Railroad and whose husband owned a shop that refused to sell products made by slave labor.

Over tea they discussed the challenges facing women. As Elizabeth recalled in her memoir, they decided "then and there, to call a Woman's Rights Convention." Because they wanted Lucretia to be a featured speaker, they planned to hold the convention quickly, within the week, before her planned return to Philadelphia. That very evening they placed an ad in the local paper, announcing "a convention to discuss the social, civil, and religious condition and rights of woman." They found a local church that was willing to host them, and they began to plan the event.

The most important order of business was to write a document to sum up the event's purpose and the organizers' concerns. They decided to use the Declaration of Independence as their model, and together they drafted a document that boldly replaced the colonists' grievances against the King with their own grievances against men.

The original Declaration indicted the British King for the "establishment of an absolute tyranny of these United States"; this new document argued that "the history of mankind" has resulted in "repeated injuries and usurpations on the part of man toward woman" and "an absolute tyranny over her." They completed a draft during that first meeting; Elizabeth edited and revised it at home over the next few days. The Declaration of Sentiments, as they called it, became the first widely published American manifesto of women's rights.

Like the original Declaration, the Declaration of Sentiments listed 18 grievances, transformed into complaints about the conditions of women. They wrote about how women were denied equal pay, the right to own property, access to higher education, jobs in fields like law and medicine, a say in the laws that govern their bodies, and—once they were married—any rights whatsoever. It also criticized men for preventing women from exercising their "inalienable right to the elective franchise"—the right to vote. And like the original, their Declaration ended with a demand, by insisting that women "have immediate admission to all the rights and privileges which belong to them as citizens of these United States."

THE WOMEN DIDN'T KNOW how many attendees to expect for their hastily planned convention. But one week after that first meeting, on the morning of July 19, 1848, about 300 people gathered outside the Wesleyan Methodist church at 10 a.m. Many who came were experienced activists in other movements. Even though the announcement had specified women only, a number of men were in attendance, and some women brought their young sons.

Elizabeth welcomed the crowd, then Lucretia spoke, urging people to consider women's rights as part of "reforms in general." Lucretia's commitment to social equality was focused not just on women, but also on the rights of *all* disadvantaged people; before her trip to Seneca Falls, she had traveled extensively to meet with a range of people, including members of the Seneca Indian tribe, newly free black men and women in Canada, and inmates at a nearby prison.

Then it was time for the Declaration of Sentiments to be introduced to the audience. Elizabeth began by reading the entire document out loud. Then she went back and reread it paragraph by paragraph, going over each resolution in detail. The crowd discussed and debated each demand thoroughly, examining whether or not it should be included in the final Declaration. The process took several hours.

ON THE SECOND DAY of the convention, even more people were in attendance. When it came time to vote on the resolutions in the Declaration of Sentiments, the demand for voting rights, or women's suffrage, was the most controversial. Even Lucretia opposed it, but for different reasons: she believed that the American political and economic system was so bound up with the evils of slavery that it must be completely restructured, and that any effort to work within the political system was a compromise with slavery, which she refused. She did come to support women's suffrage—but in 1848, while slavery still raged, voting to her meant participating in an immoral system.

The convention was on the verge of eliminating the suffrage provision when Frederick Douglass stood up. Frederick, a formerly enslaved abolitionist and famous public speaker, was perhaps the lone black person at the convention. Though he and Lucretia agreed on many things, Frederick was in favor of using electoral politics to bring about change. He delivered an impromptu yet impassioned speech and insisted that suffrage be included, declaring "that it is the duty of the women of this country to secure to themselves their sacred right to the elective franchise."

The audience was convinced, and the demand for women's suffrage remained in the declaration, but it was the only resolution that was passed narrowly. Of the several hundred people in attendance, 100 of them signed their names to the Declaration of Sentiments, just as the founders had committed themselves to their new set of principles. But unlike the original, this Declaration bore the names of 68 women, alongside 32 men.

Several decades later, Frederick reflected on what it meant for him, as a black man, to support women's suffrage in its early days. "When I ran away from slavery," he said, "it was for myself; when I advocated emancipation, it was for my people; but when I stood up for the rights of woman, self was out of the question."

WOULD ANYONE NOTICE THAT 300 people had crowded into a church in a small town in upstate New York to declare that women in America should have the right to own property, live independently, and be able to vote? Would anyone *care* about the new declaration? Elizabeth and her collaborators were certain that their efforts would be criticized, and they were right. Newspapers in numerous states picked up the story: one article called it "the most shocking and unnatural incident ever recorded in the history of womanity." It wondered, "If our ladies will insist on voting and legislating, where, gentlemen, will be our dinners . . . ?" But Frederick's abolitionist newspaper, *The North Star*, published the Declaration in full, praising the bravery of all who attended the convention. Another newspaper said that Lucretia's speech was "one of the most eloquent, logical, and philosophical discourses which we have ever listened to."

The Declaration of Sentiments helped connect the idea of "women's rights" to many other social, political, and economic facets of America, from income inequality to education to religion to the emotional toll of sexism. It sparked the movement for women's suffrage, and helped inaugurate a long and brave fight to make gender equality in American a reality.

Conditions did improve for many women in America in the decades that followed. More women gained access to higher education, to careers in law and medicine, and to greater rights within their marriages. But other rights were long deferred. It would be another 70 years before the Nineteenth Amendment guaranteed women the vote, and another 120 years until the Civil Rights Act outlawed many of the barriers still handicapping the full enfranchisement of women of color (see V Is for Voting Rights, page 135).

One outcome of the Seneca Falls convention is what came next. The authors of the Declaration closed by hoping that "this Convention will be followed by a series of Conventions, embracing every part of the country." And that's what happened: women's rights activists organized, lectured, and held women's rights conventions every year, in multiple states, for decades (with the exception of the Civil War years). Their enduring efforts moved the demands of the Declaration of Sentiments forward, shaping the American fight for suffrage and gender equality.

D IS ALSO FOR . . .

DAUGHTERS OF BILITIS: The first lesbian political and civil rights organization in the United States, founded in 1955.

DIRECT ACTION: A nonviolent form of political activism utilized during the civil rights movement.

DOMESTIC WORKERS MOVEMENT: A civil rights movement to organize domestic employees, including housecleaners, nannies, and caregivers.

DREAMers: The undocumented children and young adults brought to the US by immigrant parents who qualify for the DREAM (Development, Relief, and Education for Alien Minors) Act, and the DACA (Deferred Action on Childhood Arrivals) program.

THE DECLARATION OF SENTIMENTS boldly summed up the status of women in America at the time, and offered a far-reaching vision of what equality might look like. A century and a half later, many of the grievances it listed are still relevant.

While women in America can now vote, attend college, and own property, they have a long way to go to reach true equality. The Declaration says that women earn "a scanty remuneration" for their labor—in 2018, white American women earned just 80 cents for every dollar earned by a man. Black women earned about 61 cents to the male dollar, while Latina women earned 53 cents.

Another grievance is that men compel women to "submit to laws, in the formation of which she had no voice." Today, women still make up only 20 percent of Congress.

The Declaration argues that women are allowed in church, but are excluded "from the ministry"—this is still true of many organized religious groups, which don't allow women to preach or lead services.

The Declaration goes on to point out the unfair existence of what is now known as the "double standard" (the "different code of morals for men and women"). In the final grievance, Stanton and her collaborators claim that men work to destroy women's "confidence in her own powers, to lessen her self-respect, and to make her willing to lead a dependent and abject life." Sadly, this still holds true in many ways, as women endure harassment, disrespect, and violence in homes, on the streets, and in the workplace. And this treatment is still being resisted by activists, organizations, and viral movements like #MeToo.

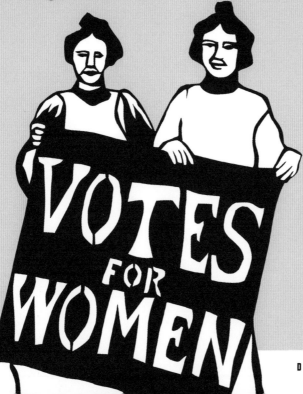

E

IS FOR
EARTH FIRST!

THE MOVEMENT TO SAVE THE WORLD'S OLDEST TREES

"You cannot seriously address the destruction of the wilderness without addressing the society that is destroying it."
—JUDI BARI, EARTH FIRST! ORGANIZER

EARTH FIRST! IT'S A rallying cry, an ideology that places the health of the planet before all other concerns. It's also the name of a radical activist organization—known as Earth First!, always with an exclamation point for emphasis—that began in the 1980s. It helped transform the environmental movement and bring national attention to the plight of some of Earth's most ancient living beings: California's coastal redwoods.

These living giants, botanical name *Sequoia sempervirens*, are the tallest trees on earth, capable of growing more than 300 feet tall. Undisturbed, they can live for more than 2,000 years. The first redwood fossils date back 200 million years, all the way to the Jurassic period. And until the 1850s, they covered more than 2 million acres along the coast of California and Oregon.

For centuries, indigenous tribes lived in harmony among the redwoods. Then came the Gold Rush, and an influx of white people. The trees provided sturdy planks for new homes: by the end of the 20th century, 95 percent of the ancient *Sequoia sempervirens* had been felled. The 5 percent of the towering giants that remain on earth are in the foggy coastal regions of Northern California. These trees don't matter just because they're beautiful, or because they used to hang out with dinosaurs. They're also part of delicate ecosystems that house numerous species of plants and animals—many of which are endangered or threatened, like the spotted owl; the marbled murrelet, a rare seabird that nests in the top branches of the trees; and the coho salmon, which swims in the many streams that run through the redwood groves.

Although decades of logging eliminated much of the old-growth redwood forest, until late in the 20th century the local family-owned lumber companies that had been in the business for generations used sustainable logging methods. These companies knew that if they wanted to continue to have trees to cut down, they must do it wisely. In 1986, one of these companies, Pacific Lumber, locally owned since 1863, was suddenly taken over by Maxxam, a huge Texas corporation. The new owner, millionaire Charles Hurwitz, needed to make as much money as possible. He tripled the timber harvest and began clear-cutting the ancient redwoods. Environmental activists in the area knew this method would wipe out the remaining trees in no time. The fight to save the ancient redwoods was on.

ENTER EARTH FIRST!, an organization founded around 1981 by a small group of men who were fed up with mainstream environmental activism, which they thought was too polite and careful. Earth First! had no real structure or single leader, and anyone who agreed with its philosophies could join. The members published their ideas in the *Earth First! Journal* and engaged in mostly secretive direct attempts to disrupt practices that were destructive to the environment, like logging and the building of nuclear power plants.

The Earth First! activists were funny and creative, often making music and theater part of their protests. They were also committed: their motto was "No compromise in defense of Mother Earth!" and they were willing to put their bodies in front of bulldozers to protect trees.

Longtime activist and union organizer Judi Bari liked this approach, and she agreed with the Earth First! philosophy of deep ecology: the idea that Earth is not here just for human consumption, but that all species have a right to exist. Judi had moved to Northern California the same year the clear-cutting began and had been making her living as a carpenter until she realized the redwood planks she was hammering nails into came from trees that had been alive for centuries. She turned her attention to the growing activism against the new clear-cutting policies and joined forces with local Earth First!

activists, quickly emerging as a powerful and charismatic leader.

But Judi didn't like everything about Earth First! Most members were macho guys focused on daring individual actions. The guys could be obnoxious and aggressive in their defense of the trees, and they didn't have a very cohesive strategy. As a feminist, Judi found this approach to be problematic: she thought big collective actions that bring lots of people together in a nonviolent way would be more effective. She wanted to be more organized, and to have a larger vision.

As she took on more of a leadership role, she convinced the Earth Firsters to commit to nonviolence, and to publicly denounce dangerous practices like tree-spiking (inserting metal spikes inside trees to destroy the blades of chainsaws) and monkey wrenching (intentionally destroying machinery or other industrial equipment). She actively recruited women to be more involved, and she did something that even the most radical activists hadn't attempted: she reached out to the loggers.

JUDI WAS AN EXPERIENCED organizer: she'd unionized grocery clerks and postal workers, helping them advocate for better wages and conditions. She was determined to use her background to change the hostile ways that environmental activists and loggers related to each other. She hung out in the local bars at night, getting to know the loggers and having conversations with them, instead of just yelling at them. Building trust between Earth First! activists and local workers wasn't easy, but Judi saw it as an essential piece of the movement's puzzle.

Judi argued that loggers and environmentalists shouldn't see each other as enemies. The real enemies were the faceless, super-rich corporations that were destroying the planet and creating unsustainable working conditions. She started a small union of timber workers through the International Workers of the World (IWW) and made connections between workers who needed jobs and couldn't afford to lose work because of protests and the people who were passionate about protecting the environment.

We *all* need a healthy planet, Judi argued. Sustainable logging practices are in everyone's best interest; if all the trees were rapidly clear-cut, what would happen to the jobs? At the same time, she worked to convince Earth Firsters that loggers are human beings, not tree-hating monsters. They had families, and they needed jobs. Yelling at them wouldn't solve the problem.

In February of 1990, Judi had an idea for a major action that would bring national attention to their efforts. That November Californians would vote on a bill called Forests Forever that would restrict clear-cutting. The timber companies had vowed to cut down as many trees as possible before November, in case the bill passed. Judi's vision was to get huge numbers of activists to Northern California to protest the destructive logging practices and slow down—or even halt—the timber harvest. With the support of many Earth First! activists, Judi announced plans for what they called Redwood Summer, and devoted the next several months to making it happen.

The model for Redwood Summer was the Mississippi Freedom Summer of 1964, when thousands of young people traveled to Mississippi to register black voters and be part of the civil rights movement. Judi and a handful of other Earth First! organizers coordinated the details for the months-long action, which would include marches and sit-ins, direct actions, rallies, guerrilla theater, and more. They recruited college students from around the country, they drew maps, established schedules, plotted routes, built basecamps, and did outreach to the media. They coordinated with other activist groups, like Food Not Bombs, who pledged to provide food for the activists.

DESPITE JUDI'S EFFORTS TO bridge the divide between activists and locals, it didn't always work. Many locals were furious at the idea of thousands of young "hippies" coming into their communities, trying to stop them from doing their jobs. Anti-Earth First! bumper stickers decorated the bumpers of trucks, and many homes displayed signs telling Earth First! to leave town. The most serious anger was directed toward Judi, her colleague Darryl Cherney, and several other leaders. They received death threats on a regular basis, and though they reported them to law enforcement, nothing much was done to investigate. It was seen as the price they had to pay for the work they were doing.

Redwood Summer was almost underway when one of those threats became reality: On May 24, 1990, Judi and Darryl were driving in Oakland, California, when a bomb exploded underneath the car, nearly killing them both. They were rushed to the hospital—and arrested while undergoing surgery. The police accused them of building the bomb themselves. Word spread that Judi Bari and Earth First! were terrorists, though everyone who knew Judi knew she was committed to nonviolence and would never go near a bomb. Prosecutors never filed any actual charges, and the Oakland police and FBI failed to find any evidence. But the damage to Judi's and Darryl's reputations had been done.

Luckily, the attack didn't stop Redwood Summer; in fact, it increased participation. As Judi and Darryl recovered, thousands of people participated in nonviolent actions in defense of the ancient redwoods. They held demonstrations at timber companies, sang songs, dressed up like spotted owls, and carried giant puppets. They chained themselves to machinery so that it couldn't be used, blocked logging roads, and placed their bodies between loggers and ancient trees. There were women-led tree-sits, in which activists sat on platforms high up in the trees, and daring banner drops, where people unfurled massive banners with protest messages above busy highways. Although the activists didn't stop the logging, they definitely brought attention to it.

At the end of the summer, people returned to homes and schools. Judi and Darryl were mostly recovered, but no one knew who had placed the bomb under their car.

In November, the Forests Forever ballot measure lost by just a few percentage points. Many of the activists felt a sense of despair, but the fight to save California's old-growth redwoods wasn't over.

Judi successfully sued the Oakland police and the FBI in 1991; she and Darryl were awarded $4.4 million. In March 1997, Judi died of breast cancer, but she remained a passionate activist up until her passing, giving interviews from her hospital bed. Redwood Summer brought awareness to old-growth forest logging, corporate power, and the relationship between social justice and the environmental movement. In 1999, the Headwaters Forest Reserve was created, preserving 7,500 acres of ancient, pristine forests.

E IS ALSO FOR . . .

EARTH DAY: An annual event on April 22 that highlights the importance of environmental protection.

ELLIS ISLAND: The former immigration station that opened between New York and New Jersey in 1892 and saw more than 12 million immigrants enter the US.

ENDANGERED SPECIES ACT: The landmark 1973 legislation aimed at the prevention of animal and plant extinction.

EQUAL RIGHTS AMENDMENT (ERA): The proposed constitutional amendment, written by Alice Paul and Crystal Eastman and introduced in 1923, that would guarantee equal legal rights of the sexes.

JULIA AND LUNA

NINE MONTHS AFTER JUDI Bari's death, another woman set out to bring attention to the redwoods. A young activist named Julia Butterfly Hill climbed up into a 1,000-year-old tree she named Luna, and she lived there for 738 days to prevent Pacific Lumber loggers from cutting it down.

Julia Hill earned her nickname when she was hiking with her family as a child and a butterfly landed on her hand—and stayed there the entire time. When she was 22 she was almost killed by a drunk driver. It took her almost a year of physical therapy to relearn how to walk and talk, and during that time she reflected on her life and purpose. She wanted to do something meaningful in the world.

During a road trip to California, Julia fell in love with the ancient redwood forests and met a group of activists who told her about the logging threats the trees faced—and what they were doing to protect them. One of their tactics was tree-sitting, where you build a small platform high up in a tree and remain there to stop it from being cut down.

Julia felt drawn to Luna, a 180-foot-tall redwood tree. In December of 1997, she agreed to do a tree-sit, and soon she was living over 100 feet off the ground on a six-foot-wide wooden platform. She planned to stay up there for a week, but once she realized how much the loggers wanted to cut Luna down, she decided she couldn't leave.

Julia lived in Luna for more than two years to prevent the loggers from destroying her, and from clear-cutting the surrounding trees. She endured cold, wind, rain, illness, and continued harassment. Helicopters flew overhead to try to intimidate her, and furious locals threatened her from the ground. Local supporters and Earth First! activists brought basic supplies, and she cooked her meals on a tiny propane stove. To stay warm, she spent most of her days in a thick sleeping bag.

She finally came down in 1999, the same year that the Headwaters Forest Reserve was finally established. A 200-foot perimeter around Luna would be entirely preserved. Julia remains a committed environmental activist. And to this day, Luna remains standing, towering nearly 200 feet above the earth.

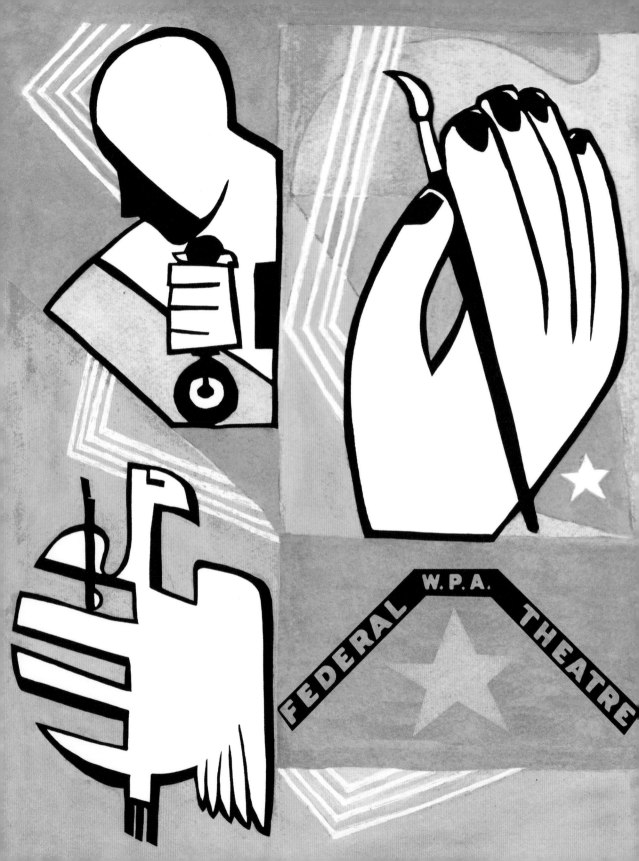

F

IS FOR

FEDERAL THEATRE PROJECT

AND THE PEOPLE WHO BROUGHT THEATER TO THE NATION

"The theater is one of the great mediums of understanding."

—HALLIE FLANAGAN, DIRECTOR OF THE FEDERAL THEATRE PROJECT

An antiwar modern dance performance based on an ancient Greek tragedy.

An all-black production of Shakespeare's Macbeth set in Haiti instead of Scotland.

A Spanish-language play about Cuban immigrants, performed in Florida.

A play about the price of electricity, based on recent newspaper headlines.

And a children's fairy tale about roller-skating worker beavers who start a revolution and attack their evil boss so they can be free to eat ice cream and be happy all day. . . .

THESE ARE JUST SOME of the wide-ranging, sometimes controversial plays produced by the Federal Theatre Project (FTP), a branch of President Franklin Delano Roosevelt's ambitious New Deal.

Between 1935 and 1939, the FTP presented more than 1,000 plays in 200 theaters in 31 states from coast to coast. It brought live performances to millions of Americans, many of whom had never seen a play before. And in the midst of a nationwide crisis of unemployment and poverty, the FTP provided jobs to thousands of actors, directors, writers, costume designers, journalists, lighting technicians, puppeteers, hair stylists, violinists, carpenters, muralists, and clowns. (Yes, clowns. The circus unit employed more than 250 out-of-work circus performers!)

The New Deal was a set of programs and policies intended to put Americans back to work after the stock market crash of 1929 and the Great Depression that followed. When Roosevelt won his election in 1932, the economy was in ruins: nearly 25 percent of white Americans were unemployed, compared to 3.5 percent in 1929. It was even worse for people who were already poor before the Depression. And those in predominantly black communities were devastated by unemployment rates of almost 50 percent. Many farmers lost their land, and food became scarce. It was a national crisis.

President Roosevelt believed that the federal government could solve the problem—and he wanted it all done *fast*. He assembled a group of smart and thoughtful people (including his wife, First Lady Eleanor Roosevelt) to brainstorm as many ideas as possible.

The New Deal resulted in many changes to how the federal government worked. In particular, it created new government agencies (often referred to as "alphabet soup" agencies, because almost all were known by their initials), including the Public Works Administration (PWA), National Youth Administration (NYA), Works Progress Administration (WPA), Tennessee Valley Authority (TVA), Civilian Conservation Corps (CCC), and more. Of these agencies, the one that employed the most workers was the Works Progress Administration (later renamed the Work Projects Administration).

Led by a social worker named Harry Hopkins, the WPA employed millions of Americans to build parks, bridges, schools, roads, and other structures. By the end of the 1930s, WPA workers had built something in almost every community in the United States. (Most of these structures still stand today. You might find a "WPA" stamp in the concrete of a sidewalk where you live.)

Harry knew that unemployed people weren't just manual laborers; they had all kinds of skills, and many were artists. So he created five programs—the Federal Writers Project, Federal Art Project, Federal Music Project, Historical Records Survey, and Federal Theatre Project—that provided jobs for more than 40,000 artists and brought art to anxious Americans in need of hope, inspiration, and information.

Of these projects, the FTP, under the guidance of a college professor named Hallie Flanagan, engaged the most people—and caused the most controversy. Hallie, the first woman to win a prestigious Guggenheim Fellowship, was a respected theater director working at Vassar College when she got a call asking her to come to Washington, DC, to talk with Harry Hopkins about "the unemployed actors." When they met, Harry offered Hallie the opportunity to create a federally funded national theater from scratch. She decided she couldn't say no.

Suddenly Hallie was armed with millions of dollars in government funding and charged with building a brand-new theater organization to entertain a nation of 128 million people. She got right to work.

HALLIE BELIEVED THAT THEATER should tell the story of every American. It should be performed not just on fancy stages but also in small towns, rural areas, and poor communities. Her plan was to start with five regional theaters: in New York, Los Angeles, Chicago, Boston, and New Orleans. From there, she would expand to other cities. Each one would be independently run by local artists who would know how best to serve the local populations. They would hire local playwrights to create new works and would tour smaller towns, encouraging residents to join them. She envisioned beautiful buildings and stages for each company, built by WPA workers.

Within the first year, more than 10,000 previously unemployed people were earning a living by writing, directing, or performing FTP productions. The plays ranged from classic Shakespeare and vaudeville to modern dramas by well-known playwrights like Eugene

O'Neill and Lillian Hellman. There were fresh adaptations of classics, like the performance of *Macbeth* done by an all-black cast at a theater in Harlem. And they premiered work by brand-new playwrights who went on to become famous, like Arthur Miller.

A POPULAR STYLE of FTP play was the Living Newspaper: researchers and journalists turned current events and newspaper articles into dramatic scripts. Audiences were entertained and informed at the same time. A play called *Triple-A Plowed Under* was based on an article about suffering farmers. The popular *One-Third of a Nation* addressed the housing crisis, with a set designed to look exactly like a New York City tenement building.

Many of the plays were explicitly political. When Hallie agreed to run the FTP, Harry had told her she'd be free from censorship. It was a promise he wasn't able to keep: though Hallie had a lot of artistic freedom, the projects ultimately depended on the approval of politicians. As the FTP became more successful, with shows selling out and critics raving about many of the performances, politicians in Congress began to pay more attention to the content of some of the plays.

Ethiopia, a Living Newspaper play about a meeting between the leaders of Italy and Ethiopia, ended up being shut down. A Seattle-based production of *Lysistrata*, the classic Greek comedy by Aristophanes, was shut down when a WPA official called it "obscene" (without actually seeing the play). Harry and Hallie fought hard against every act of censorship, even convincing Eleanor Roosevelt to step in and help them, but it wasn't always enough.

IN JUNE OF 1937, a new FTP play was about to open. *The Cradle Will Rock* was a daring "play in music" about corporate greed and labor strikes. It was also timely: sit-down labor strikes (where workers sit down at their stations and refuse to work) were becoming more and more common. *The Cradle Will Rock* drew attention to this phenomenon and to the labor movement. It was poised to be a hit; 14,000 tickets had been sold before opening night. The cast had been rehearsing for months, and the director—a 22-year-old named Orson Welles, who would go on to be considered one of the greatest film directors of all time—had built an expensive, elaborate set.

Three days before its debut, the play was canceled when the government suddenly declared that the FTP couldn't put on any new plays. Hallie, Harry, and even director Orson begged government officials to change their minds, but it was no use. The theater was padlocked, and armed guards blocked the crew from accessing the sets and costumes. But on opening night, 600 eager ticket holders still showed up, hoping the show might somehow go on.

And they were right: the determined cast and crew found another theater at the very last minute, and the audience followed them 21 blocks uptown. Out of fear that they could be arrested, the actors sat in the audience. When the curtain came up, only the playwright, Marc Blitzstein, was on stage, sitting at an old piano. He began to sing the first song of the show, and immediately was joined by another voice: the lead actor, Olive Stanton, who was standing in the audience, singing her part. The other actors did the same, and the entire play was performed spontaneously from the audience. There were no costumes, no sets, and only a single spotlight that a crew member managed to operate from the balcony. The company continued to perform *The Cradle Will Rock* this way, and it has been revived many times since.

THE FTP ALSO HAD a Children's Theater unit, which performed beloved classics like *A Christmas Carol* and *Alice in Wonderland*. The production of *Pinocchio* was seen by more than 100,000 people, including Walt Disney, who saw it eight times and raved about it. The next year, the Walt Disney studio announced their next full-length animated film: *Pinocchio*.

But not all of the children's plays were as successful. One of the most controversial was called *Revolt of the Beavers*, a whimsical fairytale about two children who travel to a land of beavers. But the beavers are oppressed, forced to work all day for a mean boss who eats ice cream and won't let the beavers have roller skates. The children help the worker beavers rise up and overthrow the boss, and they all get roller skates and ice cream and happiness. Audiences—especially children—loved it. But many critics, including members of Congress, did not: they felt it was teaching children to disrespect authority.

In 1938, a new government committee called the House Un-American Activities Committee (HUAC) formed. It was led by Texas Senator Martin Dies, who was convinced that communists and "leftists" were infiltrating American society—especially through art. Free speech mattered less than rooting out anti-American ideas, and the FTP became one of the first HUAC targets. The FTP was accused of putting on plays that were pro-union and antifascist, and that criticized segregation and discrimination against African Americans. Out of nearly

1,000 productions, HUAC singled out 81 that were "of concern." *Revolt of the Beavers* was one of them.

Hallie and others involved in the FTP went to Washington, DC, to testify before the committee and defend their work. They spoke to the power and importance of honest art. Despite it all, Congress eliminated the FTP in 1939; the other federal art projects ended soon thereafter. In her memoir, Hallie asks: "Were [the Congressmen] afraid of the Federal Theatre because it was educating the people of its vast new audience to know more about government and politics and such vital issues as housing, power, agriculture, and labor?"

While Hallie was disappointed that her time with the FTP was brief, she'd been part of something extraordinary, and she remained deeply proud of all it had accomplished. And it confirmed her belief in the power of theater: she knew that it made people think and feel.

THE LEGACY OF THE ART created in those four powerful years lived on, especially in the careers of the thousands of people who got their start as federally funded artists. In addition to the careers launched by the FTP, Harry Hopkins's Federal Art Projects provided opportunity to many of America's greatest artists, and it documented underappreciated aspects of American culture.

The Federal Arts Project commissioned more than 10,000 artists to create murals, paintings, sculptures, posters, photography, and crafts—including Dorothea Lange, Walker Evans, Jackson Pollock, Augusta Savage, and Mark Rothko. The Federal Music Project employed musicians to teach, record, perform, and even research music, which led to the field of study known as ethnomusicology. Musicians traveled the country to record African American spirituals, Appalachian folk tunes, and New Mexican folk songs. Writers Projects were established in nearly every state, and unemployed writers wrote guidebooks for their states, as well as nearly 300 books, 700 pamphlets, and 340 articles, leaflets, and radio scripts. Notable writers employed during that time include Richard Wright, Ralph Ellison, Eudora Welty, Studs Terkel, Zora Neale Hurston, and John Steinbeck.

F IS ALSO FOR . . .

FIRST AMENDMENT: An amendment to the U.S. Constitution that protects Freedom of Religion and Expression, stating "Congress shall make no law respecting an establishment of religion, or prohibiting the free exercise thereof; or abridging the freedom of speech, or of the press; or the right of the people peaceably to assemble, and to petition the Government for a redress of grievances."

FLUXUS: An art movement based primarily in New York City in the 1960s and '70s known for experimental performance art that rejected the confines and rules of traditional museum art.

FOOD NOT BOMBS: A loose-knit network of volunteers dedicated to recovering unused food and using it to cook and serve vegetarian meals to those in need.

FREE SPEECH MOVEMENT: The movement for free speech and the right to protest on college campuses that took place at the University of California, Berkeley, in 1964–65, after the university attempted to restrict the ability of students to participate in off-campus political activities.

FREEDOM RIDERS: Interracial Civil Rights activists who rode interstate buses in the early 1960s to challenge the fact that anti-segregation laws were not being enforced in certain Southern states.

IS FOR

GREAT LAW OF PEACE

THE IROQUOIS CONSTITUTION THAT INFLUENCED MODERN DEMOCRACY

This is the story of the Great Peacemaker:

Long, long ago the ancient people of the Finger Lakes made their homes on the land that is now New York. Their population grew, and soon there were five nations—the Seneca, Cayuga, Oneida, Onondaga, and Mohawk—living among the hills. They did not always get along, and they began to fight. Violent clashes made life difficult.

And then came the Peacemaker, who was also called Deganawida. He had been born to a village girl in the north, but some said he was sent by the Great Creator. Deganawida traveled from village to village, bringing a message of peace. He convinced the people of the Seneca, Cayuga, Oneida, and Mohawk tribes to cease their wars and come together as one powerful alliance.

Each nation was made up of clans, and each clan was led by several war chiefs who were selected by powerful women known as Clan Mothers. The Peacemaker convinced the chiefs to lay down their weapons and to exercise another kind of leadership: they would come together to represent their clans, to solve problems, and to display "good mindedness," a philosophy of peace and well-being. The chiefs gathered around a fire, beneath the shade of a great white pine tree whose needles grew in clusters of five. *As long as you obey the laws of peace, you will be welcome under the safe shade of this tree*, the Peacemaker explained. The Peacemaker declared the white pine the symbol of the new alliance, and he placed an eagle on its top to look out for danger.

Four nations were now united, but Tadodaho, the leader of the Onondaga people, refused to join them. He was a powerful, angry sorcerer who lived near a swamp, and had snakes in his hair. He didn't see the point of peace. He thrived on war. So Deganawida and the members of the new alliance came to Tadodaho. They approached in peace and gave him a single arrow. *Break it*, Deganawida told him. The warrior snapped it in half. Then Deganawida bundled five arrows together. *Break these*, he said. Tadodaho, known for his strength, could not break them. *This is the fate of the Five Nations*, Deganawida said. *Alone, you are weak. Come together as one and no one on earth can break your united power.*

Then Deganawida caused a solar eclipse. The darkened sun convinced the last war chiefs to accept the message of peace. Tadodaho and his war chiefs agreed to join the alliance and to listen to the Peacemaker. To reward him for changing his ways, Deganawida agreed to let the main Onondaga village (now buried beneath the city of Syracuse) be the headquarters. Tadodaho would have power, but it was the power of peacekeeping, not war.

Then the Peacemaker gathered all of the chiefs together in one Great Council. It was time to make some rules for how a peaceful, fair society should work. Using a wampum belt, he shared his vision, explaining the Great Law of Peace . . .

THIS IS ONE VERSION of the central legend of the Haudenosaunee people. While the details (and the spelling of the names) can vary depending on the translation, the basics have remained the same over several centuries. The Great Law of Peace, an oral constitution that lays out a clear structure for a fair government and peaceful society, has dictated the way of life for the Haudenosaunee for countless generations. It has also had a significant influence on American democracy.

When European immigrants first encountered the Haudenosaunee, there were 25,000 to 30,000 members in the five nations. The French called them the Iroquois; the English called them the Five Nations (and later, the Six Nations, after the Tuscarora joined in several waves of migration during the 1720s). The Indians called themselves the Haudenosaunee, which translates to "People of the Longhouse." While there were numerous Indian confederacies across the country, the Haudenosaunee were the most familiar to early American colonists in the Northeast. The Haudenosaunee's powers permeated the entire eastern half of North America (what is now the US, as well as parts of what is now Canada). It was their land that the European immigrants had colonized, and they controlled major trade routes between French and English settlements.

EARLY COLONISTS WERE FASCINATED with how the Indians lived and how they governed their large, complex societies. What stood out most was the freedom they seemed to possess. The Haudenosaunee weren't controlled by tyrannical kings, like the French and British. They didn't seem bound by wealth or money or by strict religious rules. This was shocking to some but inspiring to others.

The curiosity worked both ways. Indians observed the customs of the "white man," finding them to be just as intriguing. Indians often expressed confusion about the divisions of social classes within the colonies. Why, they wondered, did some members of the white man's society seem to think themselves

superior? Why did some have more money, and others have less—why not just share food and goods with everyone equally?

One colonist who became interested in Haudenosaunee society was Benjamin Franklin, a printer, writer, and political theorist. During the 18th century, the challenge before the colonists was great: they rejected the strict monarchy of Britain, and they needed to come up with a new way to organize a nation made up of 13 separate groups who didn't necessarily get along.

Benjamin devoted much of his life to this effort. He and the other founders looked to foreign societies—including the Greeks, Romans, and French—for ideas. But they also looked to their own neighbors, who demonstrated how once-warring nations could come together as one.

Benjamin owned a print shop in Philadelphia, and in 1736 he began printing books about Indian treaty council meetings. He spent time talking with and observing the Haudenosaunee, and he saw them as inspirational examples of liberty. (And he wasn't alone: when the Boston colonists rose up during the Boston Tea Party, they were dressed up like Mohawk Indians, whom they saw as examples of totally free people.)

In 1744 a meeting was held between the Haudenosaunee and the colonists in Lancaster, Pennsylvania. The head of the Onondaga nation, Canasatego, shared strong opinions about how the settlers should handle the tensions among the colonies. He told them "We heartily recommend Union and a good agreement between you, our brother. Our wise forefathers established unity and friendship between the Five Nations . . . We are a powerful confederacy, and by your observing the same methods our wise forefathers have taken, you will acquire fresh strength and power." In other words: *you white people would have a lot more power if you'd stop fighting with each other and figure out how to get along, as we did.*

In 1754 Benjamin Franklin arranged the Albany Congress, the first major meeting about uniting the colonies. He presented a vision for a new unified colonial government that echoed Canasatego's advice. It was rejected by the colonies, but it later became a blueprint for the Articles of Confederation, as well as the Declaration of Independence and the U.S. Constitution, all of which Benjamin would help shape decades later.

FOR SEVERAL CENTURIES THE Great Law of Peace was an oral constitution, recorded and passed down in the form of stories as well as wampum, the traditional shell beads used by the Native nations for currency, decoration, ceremony, and storytelling that transferred culture between generations. In later years the Great Law was written down and translated into Native languages and English. There are numerous written versions of it, but all have 117 articles, or rules, and are based on three main principles: peace, justice, and "good mindedness." These three values are not unlike "life, liberty, and the pursuit of happiness," the inalienable rights enshrined in the Declaration of Independence. At the time of writing this book, the Haudenosaunee Grand Council maintains a Great Law of Peace committee responsible for keeping the laws together, as well as arranging annual recitals of all 117 articles.

There are other notable similarities between the Great Law of Peace and the founding documents of American democracy, all of which are seen as the supreme law of the land and the basis for the structure of government. The Constitution, which took effect in 1789, divides the one main federal government into three branches: judicial (the Supreme Court and other federal courts), legislative (Congress, made up of the House of Representatives and the Senate), and executive (the president). It also outlines the power of individual states and their relationship to this central government. The Bill of Rights, the first ten amendments to the Constitution, details the individual liberties of Americans and places limits on government power.

The Great Law outlines something very similar. The Grand Council is the central governmental body of the Confederacy; each nation is governed separately by chiefs, who come together to make decisions and settle matters. Like Congress, they're divided into two groups: Elder Brothers and Younger Brothers. The Elder Brothers would debate issues first; once there was a decision, it would go to the Younger Brothers. If the two "houses" disagreed, the Onondaga nation would cast the deciding vote. If they disagreed, the issue would go back to the Council. Other rules guarantee fairness among the tribes and are echoed in the Constitution's emphasis on the balance of powers, and the system of checks and balances.

The Great Law protects people from unauthorized entry of homes, which is similar to the Fourth Amendment, which protects against unlawful search and seizure. It guarantees freedom of religion and the right of any person to come before the Grand Council if they have a problem, just as the First Amendment does. The Great Law also determines the official symbols of the Haudenosaunee, including the eagle placed at the top of the pine tree to look out for danger, and the cluster of five bound arrows, which symbolizes unity. The official seal of the United States is an eagle clutching 13 arrows that represent the unity of the original 13 colonies.

There are also plenty of aspects of the Great Law that the framers of the Constitution did *not* follow. While the Great Law emphasizes communal ownership of land and goods, the Constitution emphasizes private property. The Great Law is centered on consensus-based decision making, whereby all of the nations' representatives come to agreement, rather than the majority-rule method of Congress. Under the Great Law, *all* people are equal.

AND THEN THERE IS the treatment of women. America's founding documents don't mention women at all. American women had very few, if any, political rights before the 20th century, and they weren't granted the right to vote in federal elections until 1920.

In contrast, the Haudenosaunee women had great political power. Men were the appointed representatives, but they were all chosen by the Clan Mothers, who were included in all important events, like council meetings and treaty signings (this did *not* go over well with the male colonists, who were often shocked at the presence of Indian women). The Great Law states that council members can be removed if they don't listen to the admonishments of their "women relatives," and the Clan Mothers had the power to "dehorn" or impeach council members. Land sales weren't finalized until Clan Mothers approved, and they also had veto power to block war. While men and women had distinct roles, neither gender was subordinate to the other.

For these reasons, the Haudenosaunee's ways were of interest not only to early American men, but also to colonial women, who spent time with members of the clans, observing how Haudenosaunee women were revered and respected in these matrilineal societies. Early women's rights advocates used these examples as evidence that women were not "naturally" inferior to men—a common argument at the time.

In 1893 writer and women's suffrage activist Matilda Joslyn Gage was adopted into the Wolf Clan of the Mohawk Nation, enabling her to vote on tribal matters. That same year, she was arrested for attempting to vote in a local school board election. In her 1893 book, *Woman, Church and State*, Matilda argued that "the modern world is indebted" to the Iroquois "for its first conception of inherent rights, natural equality of condition, and the establishment of a civilized government upon this basis."

Americans are often taught that the first Europeans who arrived on American soil "discovered" a new world. This is just not true: there already *was* a world, a complex one filled with distinct societies, languages, religions, wars, governments, and customs. The story of the United States of America may begin with the arrival of the first European immigrants, but the story of the inhabitants of this land goes back centuries—as do so many of the core elements of American government and democracy.

G IS ALSO FOR . . .

GERMAN COAST SLAVE REVOLT: An 1811 uprising where 500 enslaved people marched toward New Orleans, burning plantations and chanting "Freedom or Death!"

GILMAN: A legendary all-ages punk club located at 924 Gilman Street in Berkeley, California; it has long been a center of activism and alternative music and culture.

GODEY'S LADY'S BOOK: An American women's magazine published in Philadelphia from 1830 to 1878 that was the most widely circulated women's magazine of the 19th century.

GREAT MIGRATION: The widespread movement of approximately 6 million African Americans from the rural Southern United States to urban cities in the Northeast, Midwest, and West between 1916 and 1970.

IS FOR
HULL HOUSE

AND THE WOMEN WHO OPENED THEIR DOORS TO IMMIGRANTS

"Nothing can be worse than the fear that one had given up too soon and left one unexpended effort which might have saved the world."

—JANE ADDAMS, COFOUNDER OF HULL HOUSE

IN 1889 JANE ADDAMS and Ellen Gates Starr bought a run-down, abandoned mansion in the middle of the poorest neighborhood in Chicago, Illinois. They moved in, began to fix it up, and soon opened the doors of Hull House, one of the first settlement houses in the United States dedicated to serving poor communities.

The settlement house movement began in England in the 1880s. A settlement house was a private home located in an impoverished community. The people who lived in the home were not poor—they were usually white, college-educated, middle-class individuals who wanted to be of service by "settling" in communities that needed assistance. The residents of settlement homes formed bonds with the community, offering services and care that local governments often failed to provide, including childcare, healthcare, and education.

When Jane learned about the settlement house movement, she knew she wanted to be part of it. She'd always wanted to do something to help others, but a severe back injury had halted her dream of becoming a doctor. After her father passed away unexpectedly, Jane inherited a huge amount of money, which allowed her to travel to London with her friend and lover, Ellen, whom she'd known since college. The two visited Toynbee Hall, a well-known settlement house there. Jane was inspired. Her vision of how to make a difference in the world became clear.

Jane told Ellen that she wanted to start a settlement home in Chicago, the booming Midwestern metropolis a few hours from Rockford, Illinois, where they'd gone to college. Chicago was a rapidly expanding center of industrialization and home to massive waves of new immigrants, many of whom were ignored by city officials and charities. The prevailing attitude at the time was that poor people in need of charity were somehow flawed. Jane wanted her settlement home to be like Toynbee Hall—but run by women rather than by men. Ellen loved the idea and committed herself to helping make it happen. They returned to the United States and went immediately to Chicago, searching for the right house in the right location. They were both 29 years old; after a decade of trying to figure out what to do with their lives, the women had found their purpose.

DURING THE SECOND HALF of the 19th century, Chicago, like many large American cities, experienced a major population boom. The first waves of European immigrants came from Germany, Ireland, and Sweden; by the 1880s, they were coming from all over eastern and southern Europe, seeking the American dream of freedom and prosperity. Many were fleeing poverty; others, especially Jewish families from Eastern Europe, were fleeing violence and persecution. Chicago was a hub for railroads, and there were jobs in lumberyards, stockyards, and hundreds of factories. But it was not an easy life. The workers had almost no protections, and worked grueling hours for low pay.

By 1890, more than 40 percent of Chicago's residents were recent immigrants, and nearly all lived in cramped, unsanitary slums on the city's West Side. City officials mostly ignored these communities, and it showed: streets were unpaved and filthy, and most of the buildings lacked plumbing and electricity. There weren't enough schools or doctors for the children, and preventable diseases spread fast. This is where Jane and Ellen found their new home, located at 800 South Halsted Street.

Jane and Ellen's vision was to create a spacious home that would feel welcoming to any person, no matter how much money they had, what language they spoke, or what country they came from. This was important, because Jane and Ellen's new neighbors were almost all recently arrived immigrants from countries

like Germany, Italy, Sweden, England, Ireland, France, Russia, Poland, Greece, Bulgaria, and the country then known as Czechoslovakia.

AFTER MOVING IN, JANE and Ellen began reaching out to women they knew, inviting them to join the new venture. The initial Hull House residents had a lot in common: they came from wealthy families, and many had fathers who were active in politics. They were part of the first generation of American women to attend college, which came to be known as the New Women of the Progressive Era.

This period in American history was marked by widespread social activism and political reform; the New Women were an elite class of mostly white women committed to social change. They took advantage of increasing opportunities in education and employment, and they focused on civic engagement and improving society. They also tended to reject the traditional expectations for young women, often choosing to remain unmarried, to not have children, and in some cases, to engage in romantic relationships with other women. Many of the Hull House leaders (as well as other prominent New Women like Susan B. Anthony and Eleanor Roosevelt) were in committed romantic partnerships with other women.

HULL HOUSE SOON HAD a team of eager residents who paid room and board and gave their time to run programs for people in the neighborhood. They taught classes, cared for children, served meals, and helped run the day-to-day operations. They weren't paid for this work—living as a Hull House resident was about being of service.

The goals for Hull House were modest at first: Jane and Ellen started offering art and literature classes, inviting their less-fortunate neighbors to learn about art history and hear Ellen read aloud from some of her favorite books. It was a nice idea, but they soon realized it wasn't enough. Their neighbors couldn't just drop everything and come look at art. The men worked constantly, and many of the women had to work too. They didn't need a poetry reading; they needed *childcare*.

So Jane and Ellen started a kindergarten. Right away, 24 children were enrolled, and more than 70 were put on a waiting list. They added a day nursery for babies, and sent teachers to the homes of children who were too ill or disabled to attend school. With their youngest children safe and cared for, neighborhood women were able to work. Eventually Hull House built an entire Children's House that included laundry and sewing facilities for mothers who didn't have access to them at home.

And this is how Hull House grew: for the next several decades, the residents and leaders listened to the needs of the community members, then adapted and expanded to serve the diverse population. They worked to understand the challenges facing immigrants, especially the women, who were often young and uneducated. They also recognized and honored the emotional challenges of living in a new country, including homesickness. Hull House hosted "ethnic nights" devoted to celebrating the food, music, and traditions of different immigrant communities. There were Greek nights, Italian nights, Polish nights, Jewish nights—and all were welcome to attend.

BY THE FIRST DECADE of the 20th century, Hull House had expanded beyond the once-abandoned mansion: it consisted of 13 buildings that served thousands of people each week. You could go to the gymnasium and try wrestling, boxing, or bowling. You could learn English, Italian, French, or Spanish. You could join a choir or a brass band, or Chicago's first women's basketball team. You could meet with a lawyer, take a shower, or get a hot meal and cup of coffee.

You could visit the Labor Museum on a Saturday afternoon and learn traditional old-world crafts from elderly immigrants: Irish women weaving blankets, Syrian grandmothers spinning flax into cloth. There was an art gallery, a theater, a coffeehouse, an employment bureau, and several libraries. There were lectures by leading thinkers like W.E.B. DuBois. And you could even go to Chicago's first and only playground, a beloved oasis that was the result of Jane's research into child development and her then-radical belief in the importance of play.

BUT HULL HOUSE DIDN'T just improve the lives of the people in the surrounding neighborhoods. It also transformed the lives of many of the young residents, acting as a springboard to launch them into lifelong careers in social reform and leadership. These ambitious women were often shut out of male-dominated fields like law, politics, and journalism. At Hull House, they could develop as leaders and innovators on their own terms.

Julia Lathrop came to Hull House when she was 30 years old. She'd gone to college with Jane and Ellen, but like many women at the time who didn't get married right after graduation, she'd returned home to care for her family. When Jane invited Julia to come to Hull House, Julia jumped at the chance, and she quickly discovered her passion: advocating for children. She focused on the plight of "juvenile delinquents" and documented cases where children as young as seven were tried as adults in criminal cases and sent to prison.

Julia helped to found the first juvenile court in the US, and after 22 years at Hull House, she went to work for President William Howard Taft as the first woman to run a federal government bureau. As chief of the brand-new Children's Bureau, she made child labor and safety her top priorities. When she resigned, she asked President Warren Harding to appoint Grace Abbott, another Hull House alum, as her replacement. Grace's sister Edith, also a longtime resident, helped shape the field of social work, and became the first female dean of a graduate school.

Florence Kelley came to Hull House in 1891 with her three young children; she was escaping an abusive husband, and the women of Hull House gave her a room, legal support to file for divorce, and a job that was right up her alley. Florence was a socialist, committed to worker's rights, and Jane sent her to investigate working conditions in the local factories. Florence was appalled by what she saw: there were children as young as three working in sweatshops. She wrote a sweeping report detailing her findings, and her recommendations led to a ban on employment for children under age 14 and a state law limiting women and children to an eight-hour workday. She became the head factory inspector for Illinois and managed a team of 12 inspectors, half of whom were women she knew from Hull House. Florence got her law degree and then led the National Consumers' League for 34 years.

Hull House residents Dr. Alice Hamilton and Dr. Rachelle Yarros were both pioneers in women's health. In 1923, they opened the second birth control clinic in America at Hull House, and Alice eventually became the first female professor at Harvard Medical School.

Ellen remained at Hull House for many years, developing art and craft programs and working to bring art into Chicago's public schools. She founded the Chicago chapter of the Women's Trade Union League and ran for local public office as a socialist. Though she and Jane ended their romantic relationship when Jane met Mary Rozet Smith (who became Jane's life partner and helped to fund Hull House), they continued to share a vision of social activism for the common good.

Jane lived at Hull House until her death in 1935. Over the years, she helped expand the settlement house movement, and by 1920 the US had nearly 500 Hull House–inspired facilities. She taught, wrote, and lectured extensively and is considered a founder of the field of sociology. Encouraged by journalist and leader Ida B. Wells-Barnett, Jane took a public stance against the horrors of lynching, and she supported Ida in her successful effort to stop the creation of segregated public schools in Chicago. Both women were founding members of the National Association for the Advancement of Colored People, and Jane was a founder of the American Civil Liberties Union as well.

And as the 20th century dawned, Jane became one of the world's leading peace activists, taking the skills she had honed at Hull House to the world stage. In 1915, as World War I was just beginning and the US teetered on the brink of entering the conflict, Jane helped lead a summit of 1,200 women from 12 nations who came together in the Netherlands to discuss how to end the war. The summit led to the creation of the Women's International League for Peace and Freedom (WILPF), and Jane was elected president.

When the US did enter the war, Jane was booed off the stage at Carnegie Hall for giving a speech opposing American intervention. Despite that, she stayed firm in her commitment to peace, and in 1931 she became the first American woman to win the Nobel Peace Prize.

H IS ALSO FOR . . .

HARLEM RENAISSANCE: The artistic, intellectual, and social movement involving the African American community living in Harlem, New York, during the 1920s; known during the time as the New Negro movement.

HARPERS FERRY RAID: An 1859 raid led by abolitionist John Brown to overtake a US arsenal and initiate an armed slave revolt.

HIGHLANDER FOLK SCHOOL: A site of leadership training for labor organizers and Southern civil rights activists—including Rosa Parks, Ralph Abernathy, and James Bevel—founded by Myles Horton in 1932.

HIP-HOP: A musical genre and cultural movement created in the 1970s and '80s by black and brown youth in the Bronx borough of New York City.

IS FOR

INDEPENDENT LIVING

AND THE DISABILITY RIGHTS MOVEMENT

"I had no choice because, as a disabled person, I was going to either have to get involved with changing the system that limited me or not participate in society."
—JUDY HEUMANN, DISABILITY RIGHTS ACTIVIST

IF YOU'VE EVER WALKED, ridden, or rolled along a sidewalk in an American city, you've almost certainly seen a curb cut: that part of the curb that slopes down gently, allowing a wheeled device to roll into the intersection. You may or may not have noticed the bumps on some of them, which let blind people know they're approaching an intersection.

If you've been in a public building—a library, post office, school, restaurant—you've seen a ramp leading to the front door. If you use a wheelchair, you've likely used it to get inside. You might also press the large button that automatically opens doors designed to a specific width so your wheelchair fits through.

If you've ever ridden on public transit, you may have noticed the hydraulic lifts that allow wheelchairs to board buses safely, the elevators down to the subway for those who can't use stairs, or the Braille placards for blind passengers. And if you've ever attended or worked in a public school, you may know someone who has a 504 plan or an IEP, which are both blueprints for how students with disabilities can be most successful in school. Maybe you have a 504 plan yourself.

All of these things are in place to protect the rights of people with disabilities. And they're all required by laws that were enacted after years of action, advocacy, and organizing by people with disabilities and their allies. They have quite literally transformed the landscape of American life. And much of it began in 1952, when a boy named Ed Roberts contracted polio.

THE VACCINE FOR POLIO, a highly contagious virus that often leads to paralysis, was discovered in 1954. Two years before that, 14-year-old Ed got sick and went from being an active, baseball-playing teenager to lying paralyzed in a hospital bed. Doctors weren't sure if he would survive the night.

Ed did survive, but his lungs were paralyzed; to breathe, he had to spend most of the day in an enormous 800-pound machine called an iron lung. He became depressed, worried that he'd never finish school or find a job. His mother, Zona, arranged a telephone correspondence setup that allowed him to listen in on his high school classes. He learned to turn pages of books with a stick he held in his mouth. He wrote articles for the school paper by dictating them to Zona, who typed for him.

Ed got his diploma and enrolled in community college, using a portable ventilator that let him leave the iron lung during the day. Zona brought him to campus every day, often asking strangers to help lift his wheelchair up over curbs and into buildings.

When Ed applied to the University of California, Berkeley, in 1962, he didn't mention his disability on the application—it didn't ask. When he was accepted, and he and Zona showed up on campus for a tour, the university officials had no idea what to do with him. They'd never had a severely disabled student before.

Campus facilities weren't accessible for wheelchairs, and his iron lung wouldn't fit into a dorm room. Ed insisted that he had a right to be there, and they finally agreed to let him live in a room in the campus hospital. A local paper ran a story with the headline "Helpless Cripple Goes to School."

Zona stayed with him for the first week, then returned home to her three other sons. She didn't visit Ed again for a month—she knew how important it was for him to negotiate his new life on his own. It was scary for Ed, but he soon realized: "I can do this. I can be free."

WORD SPREAD ABOUT THE quadriplegic young man who'd enrolled at Berkeley, and Ed was soon joined by other disabled people who wanted to attend college too. By 1969, there were 12 disabled students living together.

They bonded quickly, staying up late into the night discussing politics, racing in their wheelchairs, and playing loud music. They had aides to help them with their physical needs, like getting in and out of bed and personal hygiene, but they weren't *helpless*. Like many college students, they felt a new sense of independence.

And because this was the late 1960s in Berkeley, they were surrounded by political activism and big ideas. Disability wasn't just a medical issue, they realized. It was social and political. It was civil rights. They started to call themselves the "Rolling Quads" and became a visible presence around campus, cruising in their wheelchairs together. They didn't want to be hidden away—they wanted to be seen. And respected.

Together, they developed a core philosophy: disabled people know best how to meet their own needs; those needs can best be met by comprehensive programs that provide a variety of services; and disabled people should be integrated fully into their communities.

Based on these three ideas, they pressured the university to make the campus more accessible, and they started a small support center for disabled students. It was a success, but they wanted to do even more. They decided to create a center that would help disabled people manage their own lives.

IN 1972, THEY OPENED the first Center for Independent Living (CIL) in a rundown apartment in Berkeley. Staffed almost entirely by people with disabilities, the CIL offered everything from legal services and job placement to wheelchair repair and help finding accessible housing. It was a place where anyone with a disability could come for support, advice, and information in order to live an independent life. There was nothing else like it in the country, but soon there would be: cities all over began opening their own independent living centers.

As the CIL grew, so did the broader movement for disability rights. Members of the CIL were instrumental in getting the city of Berkeley, and then Oakland, to install curb cuts in the sidewalks of major intersections. Berkeley became a magnet for people with disabilities, gaining a reputation as a safe, accessible place to live. In 1972, there were about 400 disabled people in the city. But by 1976, there were nearly 4,000.

That same year, Ed got a new job when California governor Jerry Brown appointed him as the director of the California Department of Rehabilitation, a state agency tasked with supporting disabled citizens and shaping statewide policy. Ed was the first severely disabled person to hold the position; an employee of the same agency had once told him that he'd never be able to find a job.

ONE OF THE DISABILITY rights leaders who'd also come to Berkeley was Judy Heumann. As a child, Judy was excluded from public school because her wheelchair was considered hazardous in the event of a fire. She went on to become the first wheelchair-using public school teacher in New York, where she remained until she came to California to help run the CIL.

In 1977 Judy became a driving force behind a major moment in the fight for disability rights when she, Ed, and other activists led the charge to demand enforcement of regulatory language known as Section 504. In 1973 Congress passed the Rehabilitation Act, one of the first pieces of federal legislation to address disability. Section 504 consisted of a single sentence that had the power to change lives: "No otherwise qualified individual with a disability in the United States . . . shall, solely by reason of her or his disability, be excluded from the participation in, be denied the benefits of, or be subjected to discrimination under any program or activity receiving federal financial assistance."

Even though the Rehabilitation Act was passed in 1973, not all of the sections had been implemented through formal regulations—including Section 504. Once it did become effective, it would guarantee civil rights for disabled Americans. It would mean that any public building or institution that received funding from the government—like schools, post offices, courthouses, and libraries—would have to be made accessible. Yet four years after its passage by vote, it still wasn't actually enforceable.

Politicians worried it would be too expensive and complicated—they kept saying they would finally enforce it, but it just wasn't happening.

SO JUDY CALLED FOR a nationwide sit-in of federal buildings in ten cities. On April 5, 1977, hundreds of disabled people and their attendants and family members walked and rolled into the buildings and demanded that Section 504 be enforced. They spent the night, made their demands, spoke to the media, and returned home the next day.

Except in San Francisco, where 150 protesters did *not* go home. In fact, they remained for nearly a month, making it the longest occupation of a federal building in US history. The 504 sit-ins drew nationwide attention; most nondisabled people had never seen a gathering of this many people with disabilities. And they'd never seen them engaging in this kind of activism.

The protesters included people of all ages, from the elderly to college students to children with their disabled parents. They had a range of disabilities: there were quadriplegics, blind people, Deaf people, people with cerebral palsy and multiple sclerosis. Many had never spent a single night away from home; they relied on equipment and in-home setups, from beds with hanging straps to commodes and breathing apparatuses. Medications had to be refrigerated, some people had restricted diets, and many required full-time assistance to get in and out of wheelchairs.

They worked together with their aides and community members to convert sinks into showers, and to cover air conditioning units with tarps to create refrigerators for medications. They met daily to discuss strategies

and decided everything by consensus, meaning they discussed issues and came to agreements as a group. They slept on office furniture and on the floors until the Salvation Army donated cots and blankets. Food was provided by local community organizations, including the Black Panther Party, whose members came from Oakland every day with warm home-cooked meals. One of the sit-in participants, Brad Lomax, a disabled Black Panther with multiple sclerosis, was a key force in connecting the two powerful activist communities.

The protesters marched, rolled, sang, and gave speeches, insisting that they would not leave until their demands were met. On day 11 of the sit-in, Judy, Ed, and others took over the fifth floor of the building and declared it "a satellite office of Congress." They held a mock congressional hearing, and for hours, people gave testimonies about the barriers they faced in housing, education, and the workplace. They expressed what Section 504 would mean to them. Deaf participants leaned out of windows and used American Sign Language to communicate to Deaf supporters outside.

After the mock hearing, the protesters decided it was time to confront Congress for real. They selected 14 members to fly to Washington, DC, and meet with lawmakers in person. After they left, the remaining protesters insisted on "holding the building" until they got the results they wanted.

In DC, the protesters forced an actual congressional hearing, at which Judy gave an emotional speech, declaring that the "Outrage of disabled individuals across this country is going to continue. . . . There will be more takeovers of buildings until finally, maybe you begin to understand our position." The demonstrators followed President Jimmy Carter around town, even showing up at his church.

AND IT WORKED. On April 28, 1977, regulations implementing Section 504 were signed, and nondiscrimination became a fundamental legal right. When the activists who'd gone to DC returned, they held a huge rally in San Francisco to celebrate their success. The sit-in was over, and the participants had shown the world that they were strong, independent humans who could effect change on their own terms.

While it would take many more years to achieve the major federal legislation known as the 1990 Americans with Disabilities Act (ADA), the signing of Section 504 did result in noticeable changes across the country. More cities installed curb cuts, and public and federal buildings began installing ramps, wider doors and restroom stalls, lower counters, Braille signage, and other necessary accommodations.

Ed worked for the state of California until 1983, when he and Judy cofounded the World Institute on Disability. He remained a devoted activist until his death in 1995. Judy became a major leader in the movement, serving in positions related to disability and education under Presidents Bill Clinton and Barack Obama. The Center for Independent Living inspired a worldwide movement: there are now more than 400 CILs around the US and the world.

I IS ALSO FOR . . .

INNOCENCE PROJECT: A nonprofit legal organization founded in 1992 that works to exonerate wrongly convicted people through the use of DNA testing.

INTERNATIONAL HOTEL: Also known as the I Hotel, this was a San Francisco building and community space that provided low-income housing to Asian Americans (mainly Filipino immigrants) for nearly six decades until it was demolished by real estate developers in 1981.

INTERNET: The global system of computer networks that has transformed modern communication, enabled new modes of connection, and reshaped culture, politics, and the global economy.

J

IS FOR

JAZZ

THE SOUNDTRACK OF AMERICA

blended the instruments and melodies of their cultures.

It's the movement of people and communities—north to New York City during the Harlem Renaissance, and to cities like Detroit, Kansas City, St. Louis, Chicago, and Cleveland during the Great Migration.

In the words of Dr. Martin Luther King Jr., who wrote an essay for the 1964 Berlin Jazz Festival: "Jazz speaks for life. . . . This is triumphant music. . . . Much of the power of our Freedom Movement in the United States has come from this music. It has strengthened us with its sweet rhythms when courage began to fail. It has calmed us with its rich harmonies when spirits were down."

Here are a few moments when the "triumphant music" has been more than just song.

"What we play is life."
—LOUIS ARMSTRONG, JAZZ TRUMPETER AND COMPOSER

Jazz is more than music, more than just song and sound.

Jazz is democracy: musicians can be as free to play as they want, but they all share a responsibility to the group.

Jazz is American history, rooted in the multicultural musical traditions developed by enslaved people and immigrants.

It's New Orleans in the late 1800s and early 1900s, where people of African, French, Caribbean, Italian, German, Mexican, English, and Native American descent

"STRANGE FRUIT" AT CAFE SOCIETY
1939

IT WAS JANUARY 1939, at a New York jazz club called Cafe Society, and a woman had been singing all night. Dressed in a shimmering gown, a white gardenia tucked behind one ear, she crooned, delighting the jam-packed club with her lush voice.

It was the end of the night, time for her last song. It was a brand-new one, and she was nervous. It was so different from her other tunes, the sentimental ballads and old sad standards. This song was . . . difficult. It was intense and real.

Some people wouldn't get what it was actually about. Some would call it disgusting, and they'd walk out of clubs when she sang it. But many more would call it one of the greatest songs ever written.

The club owner wanted to make sure people really paid attention to the new song, so when the time came, he made all the waiters stop serving. No clearing tables, no pouring drinks. All the house lights were turned off, and the woman on stage was lit by a single spotlight. The crowd went silent.

The band began the intro, and she stood there with her eyes closed. One lonely horn introduced the slow melody, then the piano softly built the tune. Finally, she began to sing:

Southern trees bear strange fruit

Blood on the leaves and blood at the root

Black bodies swinging in the southern breeze

Strange fruit hanging from the poplar trees . . .

The song was "Strange Fruit," and its title and lyrics are a metaphor to describe the horrors of lynching—the devastating practice of mob murder, often done by hanging a person accused of a crime (but not found guilty in a court of law) by a noose around their neck. At least 4,000 African Americans were lynched in southern states between 1877 and 1950—and this statistic reflects only lynchings that were either reported or documented by law enforcement. Lynchings were often public spectacles, attended by huge crowds of white people. Photos of hanging bodies were published in newspapers and even made into gruesome postcards that people kept as souvenirs.

The lyrics to "Strange Fruit" never actually mention lynching, but the true meaning of

the "strange fruit" that hang from the trees becomes clear. This was part of the song's power: how it used familiar imagery to describe something almost too horrific for words.

When she finished, the spotlight went off, and she walked off the stage. No gracious bow, no "thank you" to the audience. Just the final, haunting words ("Here is a strange and bitter crop"), delivered in her signature vocal style: haunting, lingering, and always deeply emotional.

The audience was stunned. They'd been confronted, unexpectedly, with such truth. It was uncomfortable. But it was also beautiful, powerful, unlike anything they'd heard. One person clapped. Then another. And soon the room swelled with applause for the brave, wrenching honesty of the singer Billie Holiday, also known as Lady Day.

"Strange Fruit" would become her signature closing number. Some people say that the experience of singing it was so intense that she'd often go backstage and cry right afterward. It made her think about all the injustice in the country, including what her own father experienced, when he died after being refused admittance to a hospital that didn't welcome black patients.

"Strange Fruit" is the first—and only—popular song to address lynching. While it wasn't the first-ever protest song, it *was* the first political song to be performed as entertainment—not sung at a rally or on a picket line or crooned by a rabble-rousing agitator.

It was written by a Jewish schoolteacher named Abel Meeropol, a committed activist. After seeing a devastating photograph depicting the 1930 lynching of Abram Smith, Thomas Shipp, and Robert Sullivan, three black teenage boys, he wrote a poem about it. Then he set it to music, and it made its way to Billie.

After she debuted "Strange Fruit" that night in 1939 her record label refused to record it, so she took her band elsewhere and recorded it in one day. Many radio stations and clubs banned it, but it still became a hit—and a watershed moment in the history of jazz performance and social protest.

THE INTERNATIONAL SWEETHEARTS OF RHYTHM
1938

THE INTERNATIONAL SWEETHEARTS of Rhythm began in 1938, as a group of mostly orphaned teenage girls who attended Piney Woods, a vocational school in the Mississippi Delta. Within just a few years, they were playing the Apollo Theater in New York City, dazzling crowds with their tight rhythms, energetic brass section, and infectious energy.

Though many saw them as a novelty act to entertain Americans while the "real" male musicians were overseas fighting in World War II, the Sweethearts were the real deal. They featured many of the best female musicians of the day—and as a multiracial ensemble, they were the first integrated all-girl jazz band. They challenged the laws—and the attitudes—of the Jim Crow South.

Audiences were fascinated by the group's diversity. In addition to African American women, clarinet player Alma Cortez was Mexican American, saxophonist Nina de La Cruz was Native American, and trumpet player Nova Lee McGee was Hawaiian. Their original name (the Swinging Rays of Rhythm) was changed to the International Sweethearts of Rhythm to emphasize their "exotic" racial makeup.

Within a few years, the 18 band members, who were all under age 20, were crisscrossing the country in a custom-built tour bus they named Big Bertha. Experienced musicians like Ernestine "Tiny" Davis and Vi Burnside soon joined the band, and the Sweethearts became hugely popular on the "Chitlin Circuit," a network of black theaters and clubs that provided steady income for black musicians and performers. In 1941, they set a box-office record at the Howard Theater in Washington, DC, when they played for 35,000 patrons in one week.

While all of the musicians were talented, Tiny's trumpet solos were a stand-out. It's said that Louis Armstrong came to watch them play several times, and that he tried to recruit Tiny to play with him—for ten times the pay. Tiny said no; she was loyal to her Sweethearts.

Despite their popularity, touring around the South was risky. There were two white members of the band, and the fact that they were "mixing" with nonwhite people was outrageous to many white people who considered them race traitors. They also had to be careful to avoid attracting attention from police. It was even more dangerous for the nonwhite women to be in the company of two white women.

IN THE 1950S, LOUIS ARMSTRONG was one of the most famous jazz musicians in the world—and he didn't like to talk about politics. He wanted to play his music and entertain his fans. Some people, especially those in the civil rights movement, were disappointed with his refusal to speak out about racial justice and his willingness to play for segregated audiences.

All that changed in 1957, after the desegregation of Central High School in Little Rock, Arkansas, where nine black high school students had recently enrolled at the all-white Central High School to test the Supreme Court case *Brown v. Board of Education* that, in theory, had ended segregation of public schools. Despite the court's ruling, Arkansas Governor Orval Faubus ordered the National Guard to block the students from entering.

News cameras captured images of 16-year-old Elizabeth Eckford trying to enter school while crowds of white people screamed at her and the National Guardsmen stood in her way. It was on the front page of all the newspapers, and President Eisenhower wasn't doing anything about it.

At the time, Louis was in North Dakota to play a concert. Larry Lubenow, a 21-year-old local journalist, sneaked into Louis's hotel room to ask for an interview. Louis agreed, and

To avoid trouble, the Sweethearts slept and often ate inside the bus: motels in the South were all segregated, and they didn't want to deal with trying to eat in segregated restaurants. Rosalind Cron, the band's 18-year-old Jewish saxophonist, often had her bandmates apply dark makeup to her face and curl her hair before playing shows: that way, if the police came, she could try to pass as mixed-race.

After the war ended, the Sweethearts continued to play, but times had changed, and they had trouble booking gigs. The male musicians had returned, and the swinging style of the Sweethearts had begun to fall out of fashion. Most of the members moved on to other projects, though many continued to play jazz.

The Sweethearts were a mostly forgotten footnote in jazz history until a whole new audience discovered them: in 1984, feminist jazz historian Rosetta Reitz reissued a number of Sweethearts recordings on her record label, Rosetta Records, finally making them available to contemporary audiences.

even though Larry's editor told him not to ask Louis about politics, he couldn't help asking about the desegregation of Central High.

It turned out that Louis was finally ready to talk politics. And he had a lot to say. Louis let loose, his words flying fast and furious like notes from his trumpet. "It's getting almost so bad a colored man hasn't got any country," he declared. He said that President Eisenhower had "no guts" and was "two-faced." He called Governor Faubus an "ignorant plowboy" (and some other names that couldn't be printed in the *New York Times*—or in this book).

He talked about his personal experiences with racism, and admitted that when he traveled abroad "the people over there ask me what's wrong with my country." Then he dropped a bombshell: he was going to cancel an upcoming tour in the Soviet Union, because he couldn't represent a racist country.

During the 1940s and '50s, America worried about its international reputation when it came to race relations. It was hard to be seen as a beacon of democracy when images of lynchings and police attack dogs appeared in newspapers around the world. To counteract this, the government arranged a series of goodwill tours featuring popular black entertainers and athletes, like boxer Joe Lewis and opera singer Marian Anderson.

By 1957 Louis was the most famous jazz trumpeter in the world, and the U.S. State Department had arranged a high-profile trip for him to the Soviet Union. This was during the Cold War, the decades-long standoff between the two nations. The visit—and this announcement that he planned to cancel—was a *big* deal.

Larry rushed home to type up the interview. His editors didn't believe that Louis Armstrong had really said all that, so Larry came back the next day, showed Louis the article, and asked him if it was *really* what he wanted printed.

"Don't take nothing out of that story," Louis told him. "That's just what I said, and still say." Then Louis signed his name at the bottom of the article: proof that he approved.

The article ran in the *New York Times*, and was read aloud on the evening news. Some radio stations stopped playing Louis's songs as a result; one station even threw out all of his records. But others were thrilled he'd finally taken a stance.

A few days later, President Eisenhower sent members of the National Guard into Little Rock to escort the nine students safely into Central High School. Louis immediately sent a letter to the president, commending him for finally taking action.

J IS ALSO FOR . . .

JAMESTOWN: The first permanent colony of English immigrants in the Americas, it was established on land inhabited by the indigenous Paspahegh tribe. In 1619, a ship docked near Jamestown with 20 African captives, marking the beginning of the transatlantic slave trade.

JEWISH VOICES FOR PEACE: A religious organization seeking to end Israeli occupation of Palestinian land.

JUNETEENTH: The nationally celebrated holiday that commemorates the end of slavery in the US on June 19, 1865.

K

IS FOR

KOREMATSU V. UNITED STATES

AND THE FIGHT FOR THE CIVIL LIBERTIES OF ALL AMERICANS

"I was an American citizen, and I had as many rights as anyone else."
—FRED KOREMATSU, CIVIL LIBERTIES ACTIVIST

ONE DAY IN 1966, 16-year-old Karen Korematsu was sitting in her high school US history class listening to her friend Maya give a presentation about the mass incarceration of Japanese Americans during World War II. Thousands of innocent people of Japanese ancestry were put into prison camps, Maya explained. Karen had never heard anything about this history, even though she herself was Japanese American, and even though it had happened just 24 years earlier, in her own state of California. Then Maya mentioned an important Supreme Court case: *Korematsu v. United States.* Again, Karen had never heard of this—but that was *her* last name. Her classmates stared: Was it someone she was related to? Karen wondered the exact same thing.

When she got home after school, she asked her mother about what she'd heard in class. Her mother told the truth: yes, she was related to the Korematsu who sued the federal government. It was Karen's father, Fred. He had tried to show that the incarceration of Japanese Americans was wrong. Karen could not believe that her father—a quiet, peaceful man who always followed the rules and never caused trouble—would do something like that.

When Fred got home from work that evening, Karen was waiting. She asked him about the case that was so important it was part of a presentation in her own history class. Fred told his daughter that it happened long ago, that he had lost the case, but he believed he did the right thing. Karen saw the pain that came over his face. She didn't ask him any more questions that night

Until that day, Karen had not known that her own father had been among the 120,000 Americans of Japanese descent who were forced from their homes, stripped of their constitutional rights, and held in American concentration camps during World War II. And she had no idea that her own father was one of the few courageous individuals who was willing to stand up, resist, and take the fight all the way to the U.S. Supreme Court when he attempted to challenge President Franklin Delano Roosevelt's unjust Executive Order 9066.

ON DECEMBER 7, 1941, Japanese forces launched a surprise attack on Pearl Harbor, an American naval base in Hawaii. More than 2,000 Americans were killed, and the next day, President Roosevelt declared war against the country of Japan, officially entering the US into World War II. Right away, government officials began arresting various leaders in Japanese American communities, including Buddhist priests, prominent business owners, and newspaper editors. In the weeks that followed, some Americans began to worry that people of Japanese descent living in the US might be spies.

The suspicion was completely unfounded, as no person of Japanese ancestry in the United States had ever been convicted of spying. But as war hysteria continued, combined with existing anti-Asian racism, things just got worse. Government and military leaders became convinced that Japanese Americans were enemy agents. One government figure who resisted this fear-mongering was Eleanor Roosevelt, America's First Lady. Immediately after the bombing of Pearl Harbor, she flew to the West Coast to assess the situation, and publicly defended Japanese Americans on her popular weekly radio program.

On February 19, 1942, it was clear that wartime paranoia had reached the top levels of the American government. President Roosevelt signed Executive Order 9066, which authorized the military to designate areas "from which any or all persons may be excluded . . . as deemed necessary or desirable." This area was basically the entire West Coast, stretching from Washington down to California, and even extending inland to parts of Arizona. It is also where the vast majority of Japanese Americans lived.

While the order did not mention Japanese Americans specifically, it ultimately authorized the military to round up and remove 120,000 people of Japanese descent from their homes and force them into prison camps, which had been hastily set up on abandoned race tracks and fairgrounds.

The majority were American citizens—under EO 9066, their constitutional rights suddenly disappeared. Military officials argued that because America was at war with "the Japanese empire," all people of Japanese descent living in America were potential threats. Little children were threats; elderly people were threats. Farmers, florists, doctors, fruit growers, school teachers: all threats.

The announcement of the executive order took Eleanor Roosevelt by surprise, and she was not happy with the president. She attempted to talk to him about it, but in a rare show of resistance to his influential and trusted wife, he refused. She tried meeting with several of his advisers to get them to convince him to not go through with it, but it was no use. The mass removal of Japanese Americans would take place.

FRED KOREMATSU WAS 23 years old and living in Oakland, California, at the time. Fred was *Nisei*, meaning he was born in America to parents who had immigrated from Japan in the early 1900s. His parents were known as *Issei*, or first-generation Americans who had immigrated from Japan. Like many *Nisei*, Fred and his siblings were raised to be proud Americans. And like many Japanese Americans, Fred was shocked by the executive order. Yes, he was of Japanese ancestry, but he was also American. He'd been a Boy Scout, he played American sports, and he loved American music. He hardly even spoke Japanese!

When the time came, Fred's parents and brothers did what nearly every other person of Japanese descent on the West Coast did: they followed the orders, leaving behind homes, jobs, lives. "Evacuees," as they were called, had almost no time to pack, and they could take only what they could carry. Fred's family reported to the Tanforan Assembly Center, a temporary camp set up at a racetrack near San Francisco, where families were forced to live in former horse stalls. But Fred did not go. He refused to obey the unjust order.

His plan was to stay with his Italian American girlfriend, Ida. Their families already disapproved of their mixed-race relationship, and at that time in California it was illegal for a white person to marry a person of a different race. But Fred and Ida didn't care. To avoid "relocation" Fred changed his name to "Clyde"

and began telling people his ethnicity was Spanish and Hawaiian. He even underwent minor surgery to alter the shape of his eyes so he would look "less Japanese." But these desperate measures failed: Fred was arrested on a street corner and put in jail.

IT WASN'T LONG BEFORE Fred was visited by Ernest Besig, a lawyer from the American Civil Liberties Union (ACLU), an organization that believes in protecting the rights of *all* Americans. Ernest, who was white, was outraged by what was happening to Japanese Americans, and he was searching for someone brave enough to be part of a lawsuit to challenge the constitutionality of the incarceration of Japanese Americans.

While Fred was in jail, a district judge convicted him of defying military orders. He was sent to Tanforan, where he was reunited with his family—but it wasn't exactly joyous: they didn't approve of his resistance, and neither did many others. He was shunned by some fellow inmates, either because they didn't agree or because they didn't want to risk appearing disloyal by being friendly with him. Ida wrote Fred one final letter: she could no longer communicate with him, for fear of getting into trouble.

Eventually, with the help of Ernest and the ACLU, Fred appealed the case, with the hope that it would eventually get to the U.S. Supreme Court, the highest and most powerful court in the country. It would take two long years for this to happen. In the meantime, Fred and his family were relocated from Tanforan to a hot, dusty incarceration camp in Topaz, Utah.

Finally, in October 1944, Fred's case reached the Supreme Court: it was called *Korematsu v. United States.* In front of the nine justices,

Fred's lawyers argued that his arrest violated his constitutional rights, and that he was a victim of racial discrimination. The government's lawyers argued that the military believed there was a real risk of Japanese Americans on the West Coast sending information to enemy ships in the Pacific. There wasn't time, they argued, to figure out which Japanese Americans were loyal Americans and which were not. Rounding them *all* up and imprisoning them, the lawyers claimed, was the only option.

ON DECEMBER 18, 1944, the court announced its decision. Three of the nine Supreme Court justices agreed with Fred—but six of them did not. The court sided with the government, with the majority agreeing that the removal of people of Japanese ancestry was a "military necessity." The three dissenting judges strongly disagreed; they saw a clear violation of Fred's constitutional rights. Justice Robert Jackson wrote that "Korematsu was born on our soil. . . . The Constitution makes him a citizen of the United States." He also wrote that once the Supreme Court rules in favor of some form of racial discrimination, "The principle then lies about like a loaded weapon ready for the hand of any authority that can bring forward a plausible claim of urgent need."

Justice Frank Murphy's dissent was the most impassioned. He wrote that "Racial discrimination in any form and in any degree has no justifiable part in our democratic way of life. . . . All residents of this nation are kin in some way by blood or culture to a foreign land. Yet they are . . . part of the new and distinct civilization of the United States." Japanese Americans like Fred, he argued, are "entitled to all the rights and freedoms guaranteed by the Constitution."

Despite these strong words, the Supreme Court upheld the constitutionality of Executive Order 9066, and Fred lost his case. He was devastated, but he moved on with his life. The camps were shut down once the war ended. Fred had traveled to Detroit, Michigan, and there he met and married Kathryn, a Caucasian woman from South Carolina. Together they moved back to California, along with thousands of other Japanese American families who struggled to rebuild their lives. Many of the people who had been held in the camps had lost everything while they were gone: homes were foreclosed or sold (often at white-only auctions for very low prices), businesses shut down, jobs went to someone else. It was especially hard for Fred to find good-paying work because he still had a federal criminal conviction on his record.

THOUGH FRED AND KATHRYN believed that he'd done the right thing, and secretly hoped for the chance to reopen the case, they almost never spoke about it. This wasn't unusual—most Japanese Americans avoided discussing it. It was too painful and humiliating, and they just wanted life to get back to a new normal. Plus, there were still people in the Japanese American community who resented *Nisei* like Fred, who'd resisted the orders or tried to challenge the government. That's why Karen had no idea what her father had done—and was so surprised to learn the truth about her father's fight.

But time passes, and cultural beliefs can grow and evolve. In 1976, four decades after the signing of Executive Order 9066, President Gerald Ford officially rescinded it, issuing a proclamation titled "An American Promise" that called the mass incarceration of Japanese Americans a "setback to fundamental American principles."

And in the early 1980s, legal teams reopened three cases—including Fred's. Researchers had discovered documents showing that the US government knew Japanese Americans posed no threat to America during the war. The documents proved that government attorneys withheld and destroyed evidence favorable to Japanese Americans, and introduced false claims that Japanese Americans were security threats. The lawyers presented this information, and finally, on November 10, 1983, a federal court overturned the conviction of Fred Korematsu.

Fred was no longer a felon—in fact, as word got out about his story, he came to be seen as a civil rights hero. In 1988 the advocacy of the Japanese American community finally resulted in a formal apology from President Ronald Reagan, as well as payment of $20,000 to every surviving US citizen or legal resident immigrant of Japanese ancestry incarcerated during World War II.

In 1998 President Bill Clinton gave Fred the Presidential Medal of Freedom, and in 2010, California declared January 30 (Fred's birthday) Fred Korematsu Day of Civil Liberties and the Constitution—it's the first day in US history to honor an Asian American, and it is intended to celebrate the Constitution and the civil liberties of all Americans.

In 2009, Fred's daughter, Karen, founded the Fred T. Korematsu Institute, a national nonprofit organization that works with K–12 and college students and the public to promote civic education and participation. Karen is committed to carrying on her father's legacy and sharing his story to illustrate the importance of civil liberties, freedom, and human rights for *all*.

K IS ALSO FOR . . .

KAHO'OLAWE NINE: Nine activists who briefly occupied the Hawaiian island of Kaho'olawe in 1976, in an attempt to reclaim it and protest its use as a bombing range by the U.S. Navy.

KALAMAZOO CORSET COMPANY STRIKE: A historic 1912 labor strike by 500 women workers demanding fair and honest treatment.

KING PHILIP'S WAR: Also known as Metacom's War, this armed conflict from 1675 to 1678 pitted English colonial immigrants against several indigenous American tribes: the Wampanoag, Nipmuck, Narragansett, and Pocumtuck. It was the deadliest war in colonial American history and is seen by some historians as the last major effort by indigenous Americans to drive colonists from their lands.

IS FOR
LIBRARIES

AND THE FREEDOM TO READ

"Libraries are a cornerstone of democracy—where information is free and equally available to everyone. People tend to take that for granted, and they don't realize what is at stake when that is put at risk."

—CARLA HAYDEN, FOURTEENTH LIBRARIAN OF CONGRESS

MORE THAN 210 MILLION Americans use America's 17,219 public libraries every year. Libraries are more than just a place to read and borrow books: they are sanctuaries of free thought and speech. Libraries have shaped the lives of millions of Americans, and play a crucial role in protecting the rights of Americans to think, speak, and learn freely.

Public libraries—like public schools, public lands, and public property—are open to *everyone.* You can walk into a library, take a book off a shelf, and read. You can sign up for a library card, check out that book, and take it home. You can use computers to access the internet to check email, apply to college, look for jobs, do research, and more. You can take free classes and workshops, see films, and join discussion groups. You can bring children to story time. And you don't even have to set foot in a library to access information—many books and videos can be accessed online!

In America's early days, if you were not a wealthy man, books were not easy to come by. They were expensive and rare, and up until the mid-1700s they had to be shipped to the colonies from Europe. The books that did exist here were mostly religious texts printed in Latin. The earliest American libraries, like the Library Company that Benjamin Franklin and a group of men founded on July 1, 1731, were subscription libraries, accessible only to those who could afford to pay. By the middle of the 19th century, there were several public libraries in New England, and by the early 20th century, there were thousands of public libraries in America.

From the beginning, libraries were intended to be community gathering places. Andrew Carnegie, an American millionaire who financed the construction of 1,795 public libraries in the US during the early 20th century, insisted that a community room be included in every new library. He envisioned libraries as more than places to get books and information; they should be places for people to exchange ideas and connect.

WHILE IT WAS MEN like Benjamin Franklin and Andrew Carnegie who played major roles in the development of American libraries, it has long been women who have led the day-to-day operations of libraries—and shaped the role libraries play in society. Beginning in the early 1900s, *librarian* was one of the very few career choices a white middle-class woman might consider (other options included teacher, social worker, secretary, or nurse).

The list of trailblazing women in library history is long and fascinating, including ones who have pioneered innovative ways to get books to as many people as possible. One of the first bookmobiles was started in 1904 by Mary Lemist Titcomb, who worried that her library in Maryland wasn't reaching enough people. She designed a horse-drawn wagon with shelves that she could drive to rural areas of the Blue Ridge Mountains to provide books to children and families living on farms.

During the Great Depression, the Pack Horse Library Project delivered books to parts of rural Appalachia and Kentucky. Run as a federal WPA program by a woman named Ellen Woodward, the Pack Horse Project paid what they called "book women" $28 a month to spend their days riding (on their own horses or mules) to homes and schools in remote areas where there was often no electricity or running water. They brought books—and joy—to struggling communities and often provided reading lessons to largely illiterate populations.

IN THE EARLY 1900S, a young woman named Ernestine Rose began working at a Carnegie-built library on New York City's Lower East Side. Her branch was located in the midst of a large community of Chinese immigrants,

and Ernestine, who was white, felt that the library's collections should reflect that. She ordered books in Chinese and in languages of the other ethnic groups living in the neighborhood, including Russian, German, and Italian. She wrote articles explaining her multicultural vision, arguing that a library staff must understand the "history, traditions, and literature of each nationality that the library expects to serve."

During the 1920s, Ernestine became the head librarian at the 135th Branch Library in Harlem, developing programs specifically intended to bring diverse community members together; she was one of the first librarians to hire an integrated staff. This was during the Harlem Renaissance period, and many notable figures spent time in the library, including Langston Hughes and Zora Neale Hurston.

One of the staff members Ernestine hired was a young black Puerto Rican woman named Pura Belpré; she was the first Puerto Rican librarian in New York City, and most likely in the entire country. Pura devoted her 45-year library career to engaging, supporting, and entertaining *all* of the children in her communities—including the ones who spoke Spanish. Pura offered story times, puppet shows, and cultural events in both English and Spanish. New York City had experienced a large wave of immigrants from Puerto Rico, and by including traditional Puerto Rican folklore in her presentations, she helped children who were new to mainland America feel welcome and connected to their heritage. She also introduced non–Puerto Rican children to rich traditions and stories. By doing community outreach and offering multilingual, culturally diverse programming, Pura made New York City libraries feel welcoming—and showed other libraries the value of inclusive programming.

DURING THE LATE 1940S and early 1950s, America experienced a Red Scare—widespread anxiety about the communist and anarchist ideas of many people in Russia. Their views were considered dangerous to American democracy, and many American politicians became consumed with eliminating any suspected source of pro-communist ideas—from movies to musicians to books. This nationwide fear is also referred to as McCarthyism, after Joseph McCarthy, a Wisconsin senator who argued that the US had been infiltrated by Russian spies and communists, and accused countless artists, professors, journalists, and government employees of being anti-American.

One of the many repressive acts during this time was the censoring of books that were sent to US-funded libraries in countries around the world. Books by authors who were considered "un-American" were removed from libraries from Berlin to Bombay. While American libraries weren't officially ordered to remove the books, many did so out of fear.

In response, the American Library Association (ALA) issued the Freedom to Read statement in 1953. It begins, "The freedom to read is essential to our democracy," and argues that librarians should be allowed "to make available the widest diversity of views and expressions, including those that are unorthodox, unpopular, or considered dangerous by the majority."

ONE LIBRARIAN WHO FELT the impact of McCarthy era paranoia was Ruth Brown of Bartlesville, Oklahoma. In July 1950, Ruth was fired as the head librarian after 30 years in her career. She was accused of distributing communist material, but her dismissal was also likely due to her commitment to racial justice in her small Midwestern town.

Although public libraries are supposed to be free and open to all people, that has not always been the case—especially in segregated Southern states where many public libraries refused entry to African Americans. In 1939 a report showed that only 99 of 774 public libraries in the South were integrated and accessible to nonwhite patrons. Ruth, who was white, ensured that her library in Oklahoma was open to all—and that practice did not go over well with some white members of her community.

In 1945 she read the book *Black Boy,* a memoir by Richard Wright. She was moved by a scene in which young Richard, who is African American, pretends to check out books for a white man in order to use the library. She wondered how anyone could deny a person access to books and information based on the color of their skin. So she began to push harder to ensure equality in her library and her town. She started a chapter of the non-violent civil rights organization Congress on Racial Equality (CORE). She purchased subscriptions to popular black magazines like *Ebony*, and she tried to offer an integrated children's story time. She helped organize a talk by gay civil rights leader Bayard Rustin, and brought nonwhite friends to church with her. When she and two black teachers went to lunch at a segregated diner and then refused to leave when they were denied service, some in the community decided they'd had enough of Ruth.

In February 1950, just a week after Senator McCarthy began his explosive accusations in Congress, a committee of 40 citizens charged

Ruth with providing subversive materials in her library. A months-long investigation ensued, including every single book and magazine in Ruth's library. After it was discovered that the library subscribed to a publication called *Soviet Russia Today,* Ruth refused to cancel the subscription or apologize, and she defended the right of her patrons to have access to information. This refusal was considered insubordination, and she was fired. While she was accused of bringing anti-American ideas into the library, Ruth always believed that the true reason for her firing was her resistance to racism. A statue in her honor now stands at the Bartlesville Library.

IN 2001 THE ROLE of the library as a space for free speech and protected civil liberties was tested once again. After the terrorist attacks of September 11, 2001, Congress passed the PATRIOT Act, a broad statute that greatly expanded the ability of law enforcement to gain access to the information and private records of Americans. It's a long and complicated piece of legislation, but Section 215 applied to libraries: it gave law enforcement agencies expanded authority to obtain library records (including which books people have checked out), and to secretly monitor electronic communications (emails that people have sent using library computers, as well as websites people have browsed). The law also made it illegal for libraries and librarians to inform their patrons about any of this.

For most librarians, protecting the privacy of the people who use their libraries and check out books is crucial. They don't want people worrying about getting in trouble for checking out a book on a controversial or sensitive topic, especially since libraries tend to serve populations that are more likely to be considered suspicious to law enforcement and

government officials: poor people, people of color, immigrants, political activists, and formerly incarcerated people.

In the wake of September 11, American Muslims—and many people who merely looked stereotypically Muslim (due to skin color, facial hair, head coverings, and other forms of traditional clothing)—were harassed, detained, and even violently attacked. Librarians worried about their Muslim patrons: What if checking out a novel ended up leading to an arrest? What if a student doing research was suspected of being a terrorist because of the websites he accessed?

The ALA called the PATRIOT Act "a present danger to the constitutional rights of library users." By openly defying Congress, librarians risked appearing unpatriotic for criticizing government attempts to protect American safety, and they also risked losing their funding, as Congress controls federal library

budgets. But many librarians felt that this issue struck at the core of what American libraries should and should not be.

So librarians got creative. The rules said that if the FBI requested information about a library patron, it was against the law for a librarian to ever speak about it. But some librarians reasoned that they *could* say that the FBI had *not* requested information. In some libraries, employees began posting signs that hinted to patrons that their records might be under surveillance without coming right out and saying it. One sign read, "The FBI has not been here today. But watch closely for this sign to be removed."

Other librarians decided the best way to protect privacy was to have nothing at all to protect—after a book was returned, the record was deleted from the system, and many libraries began shredding paper records every day. When the attorney general of the United States dismissed the librarians' concerns about the threats to privacy and civil liberties, Carla Hayden, then president of the ALA and now the first woman and African American to become the Librarian of Congress, said, "What the library does is protect the rights of all people to fully and freely access information and to pursue knowledge, without fear of repercussion." That has been the mission of the public library for more than a century, and the minds of America are better for it.

L IS ALSO FOR . . .

LATINX: A gender-neutral term used to describe a Latino/a individual or the Latino/a community. The *x* replaces the traditional Spanish *o* or *a* ending, which identifies a person as either male or female. The term began to be used in the early 21st century, often by queer, nonbinary, and gender-nonconforming people, and those who wish to identify in a gender-neutral way.

THE LIBERATOR: An American abolitionist newspaper founded by William Lloyd Garrison that advocated for the "immediate and complete emancipation of all slaves."

LOVING V. VIRGINIA: The 1967 U.S. Supreme Court case that unanimously struck down miscegenation laws (forbidding mixed-race marriage) as unconstitutional.

M

IS FOR
MARCH!

AND THE PEOPLE WHO TAKE
TO THE STREETS

THE FIRST AMENDMENT OF the Constitution guarantees five rights: freedom of religion, freedom of speech, freedom of the press, freedom to petition the government for a redress of grievances, and freedom to assemble peaceably. When people come together to march in public spaces, to chant, sing, and hold signs expressing their beliefs, they're exercising these fundamental American rights.

Marches have been a popular tactic of American social and protest movements for centuries; they're often part of broader strategies for change-making—including organizing, lobbying, and voting—and can be especially useful for getting public attention and support. While marches alone don't always result in immediate change, they can absolutely make a big impact.

The stories that follow are only a *few* of the many notable marches in American history.

MARCH FOR WOMEN'S SUFFRAGE
1913

ON MARCH 3, 1913, more than 5,000 women marched through the streets of Washington, DC, in support of women's suffrage. It was the first major march of the suffrage movement—and the first major political march in the nation's capital.

Spearheaded by suffrage activists like Alice Paul and Lucy Burns, the march was intended to revitalize the suffrage movement and bring attention to the demand for a Constitutional amendment enfranchising women. They planned the march for the day before the inauguration of newly elected President Woodrow Wilson to take advantage of the huge crowds in town for that event, and to make sure the new president knew how serious they were about demanding the right to vote.

The organizers planned quite a spectacle, with 20 floats, 9 marching bands, 4 brigades of women on horseback, and numerous contingents of women from different countries, states, and colleges. At the very back of the parade was a contingent of men who supported women's suffrage.

At the front of the procession was labor lawyer and suffrage activist Inez Milholland. Wearing a gold tiara and flowing cape, she rode on a white horse and waved a banner that proclaimed FORWARD INTO LIGHT. Behind her was a wagon with a huge sign that read: WE DEMAND AN AMENDMENT TO THE UNITED STATES CONSTITUTION ENFRANCHISING THE WOMEN OF THE COUNTRY. Delegations of women represented different professions, including farmers, homemakers, teachers, lawyers, business-women, writers, doctors, social workers, and librarians.

The parade also reflected some deep divides within the suffrage movement—especially over race and the inclusion of black women, who worked just as hard for suffrage as their white counterparts, but often found themselves shut out, ignored, or dismissed. Ida B. Wells-Barnett, the trailblazing jour-nalist, anti-lynching crusader, and founder of the Alpha Suffrage Club, was there at the parade and had every intention of marching with her Illinois delegation. But some of the white organizers, including Alice, were either nervous or outright opposed to including black women in the procession. They didn't want to upset politicians and white women from the segregated Southern states, whose votes were needed to pass a constitutional amendment. As a compromise, the march organizers asked black participants to march in a segregated section toward the back of the parade.

Ida had traveled from Illinois as the only black member of the state contingent. On the morning of the parade, they were told that Ida would have to march separately. She refused to comply, and once the parade was underway, she snuck back into her rightful place to march between Virginia Brooks and Bell Squire, two white allies who supported her inclusion.

It's estimated that more than 250,000 people lined the streets to witness the suffrage parade, though not all of the spectators were supportive. Some angry onlookers verbally harassed the women, spit on them, threw lit cigarettes, and tried to grab banners and climb onto moving floats. Groups of men rushed forward to block parts of the pro-cession, causing stampedes and numerous injuries to the participants. The police did lit-tle to stop it, with some officers joining in the taunting, telling the marchers they should've stayed home.

Despite the injuries and insults, the women pressed on, determined to complete the parade route. The famous deaf-blind speaker, author, and activist Helen Keller had been scheduled to speak at the end of the march, but the chaos was too overwhelming, and she canceled her talk for fear of personal safety. In response to the harassment, journalist and parade attendee Nellie Bly wrote an arti-cle boldly headlined "Suffragists Are Men's Superiors." Many newspapers reported on the violence and harassment, which ended up generating sympathy for the suffrage activists and bringing more attention to the movement.

Just over 100 years later in 2017, women and their allies gathered once again in Washington, DC—and all over the world!—on the eve of a presidential inau-guration, to take a stand for the rights of women. Organized by a powerful team of women in the few months after the November 2016 election, the Women's March brought more than 700,000 people together in the nation's capital to hear from leaders like Angela Davis and Gloria Steinem, and to let the newly elected president know that they would not stand for policies that endanger women, families, and the planet.

These messages were echoed by more than three million people who marched in 400 cities across America, and seven million who marched worldwide.

The 1913 suffrage parade was the first march on Washington, DC—and the 2017 Women's March was the largest single-day protest in American history. It motivated thousands of women to get involved in activism, including many who decided to run for political office. And like the 1913 march, it reignited a feminist movement, reminding the public that the promise of America has not yet been extended to all citizens.

SILENT PARADE

1917

MANY MARCHES USE CHANTS, songs, music, and other sounds to deliver messages and engage crowds. But on July 28, 1917, when 10,000 people walked down Fifth Avenue in New York City, the only sounds to be heard were the soft shuffles of feet, coupled with the slow, steady beat of muffled drums.

It was a striking visual: women and children led the parade, dressed from head to toe in white, to signify innocence. Behind them marched men, wearing dark suits to represent the mourning of black communities. Their banners carried bold, urgent messages: THOU SHALT NOT KILL and MAKE AMERICA SAFE FOR DEMOCRACY.

The march was in response to waves of anti-black violence that were sweeping the nation, from Waco, Texas, to Memphis, Tennessee. The march was organized by the National Association for the Advancement of Colored People (NAACP), and though many NAACP members were white, it was decided that only black people would march. White allies helped organize the event, and they stood in silent support along the route.

Just three months prior to the march, in April 1917, President Woodrow Wilson had declared war against Germany and entered America into World War I, stating that he wanted to make the world "safe for democracy." The NAACP leaders saw the irony in this: President Wilson wanted America to fight for peace in other countries, but there wasn't even peace in America—not for black Americans, anyway. Public lynchings and violent attacks against black individuals, businesses, and entire communities were still taking place, including the 1916 lynching of teenager Jessie Washington in Waco, and the devastating St. Louis race riots.

Back in New York City, the leaders of the NAACP felt it was time to take action. How could America declare itself a champion of peace and democracy when its own citizens were being lynched? The NAACP called for a march, and lead organizer James Weldon Johnson had the idea to make it silent. He wanted it to feel somber, like a funeral procession to honor the dead, and to force onlookers to think about what had happened. Silence, James argued, could be even more powerful than shouts and chants. The 10,000 marchers offered an urgent reminder that America itself was "safe" for only some of its citizens.

The Silent Parade was the first mass demonstration of its kind, and it inspired many more silent protests in the years to come. After the march, the NAACP delivered an anti-lynching petition to officials in Washington, DC. These actions did not end anti-black violence by any means—in fact, lynchings and attacks on black communities increased over the next several years, including the Red Summer of 1919, the 1921 Tulsa race riots, and the Rosewood Massacre of 1923. However, the Silent Parade did raise the visibility of the issue, and it is credited with setting the tone for the many civil rights marches that would come several decades later.

BONUS ARMY MARCH

THREE YEARS AFTER THE devastating stock market crash of 1929, 25 percent of the US adult population was unemployed, including many veterans who'd fought in World War I. The people who were out of work were hungry and growing increasingly desperate.

Walter Walker, a former army sergeant from Oregon, had an idea: in 1924, Congress had issued bonus certificates to all WWI veterans, promising to pay them $1.25 for every day they had served in the war—but not until the year 1945. That was too long to wait, Walter decided; Congress should pay that money *now*. He stood up at a veterans' meeting in Portland, Oregon, and called on unemployed vets to head to Washington, DC, to demand their pay. And people listened.

Soon Walter headed east with 250 other vets, and word of the Bonus March spread fast. During May and June 1932, almost 25,000 jobless vets from 48 states took up the call and walked, hitchhiked, drove, and train-hopped their way across the nation. Many brought their wives and children with them. Newspapers and radio programs covered the trek favorably, and sympathetic train conductors—many of them vets themselves—often let Bonus Marchers ride for free. In towns across the country, people cheered on the marchers, donating food, shelter, and support.

The first contingent arrived in DC on the evening of May 21. The police chief described seeing "a bedraggled group of seventy-five or one hundred men and women marching cheerily along, singing and waving at the passing traffic." They carried signs and banners, and one man waved an American flag.

They headed to an area along the Potomac River, across from the Capitol Building. They set up camp and declared that they wouldn't leave until Congress gave them the money they were owed. Over the next month, the Bonus Army camp turned into a mini-city, becoming the largest "Hooverville" in the country. ("Hoovervilles," named for President Hoover, were large encampments of unemployed and unhoused Americans that sprang up in many cities during the Great Depression.)

The camps were ramshackle but organized: shelters were made of scrap metal, cardboard, newspaper, and other scavenged materials, but they were arranged into neat rows with street names and signs. A community kitchen fed everyone, and soon they had a post office, library, and barbershop, and a classroom for the children. Local residents who brought food and supplies included the incredibly wealthy heiress Evalyn McLean, who purchased 1,000 sandwiches and cups of coffee for the first wave of marchers. The camps were also notable for being racially integrated: black and white veterans and their families lived alongside each other—during a time of racial segregation and Jim Crow laws, this was pretty remarkable.

For more than a month, the Bonus Marchers held rallies, gave speeches, and led peaceful marches through the streets. They implored Congress to help them, and despite President Hoover's objections, the House finally passed a bill to pay out the bonuses. When the Senate failed to pass it, the veterans grew agitated. Tensions increased, and President Hoover became determined to get rid of the Bonus Army. Finally, on July 28, Hoover ordered General Douglas MacArthur to clear the streets. Five military tanks rolled down the DC streets, and hundreds of troops marched in, wearing gas masks and carrying weapons. They threw tear gas grenades into the camps, which quickly went up in flames. Veterans and their families fled the camps, under attack from their own president. Two vets and a baby were killed, and hundreds were injured.

Three months later, President Hoover was defeated by Franklin D. Roosevelt; in 1936, Congress voted to begin issuing the bonuses, and veterans were able to cash their checks. And in 1944, Congress passed the GI Bill of Rights, one of the most significant pieces of social legislation in the 20th century. It promised education, opportunity, and stability for veterans.

THE BIRMINGHAM CHILDREN'S MARCH 1963

TWO OF THE MOST notable marches of the civil rights movement were the 1963 March on Washington for Jobs and Freedom, organized by openly gay activist Bayard Rustin, where 250,000 people heard Dr. Martin Luther King Jr. deliver his "I Have a Dream" speech; and the 1965 Selma to Montgomery march, where men, women, and children were brutally assaulted on Bloody Sunday as they tried to cross the Edmund Pettus Bridge in Alabama. Both of these iconic events helped galvanize the civil rights movement—and so did the courage of the young people in Birmingham, Alabama.

In 1963 the intensely segregated city of Birmingham was ground zero for civil rights activity. Movement leaders developed a plan to integrate the city, but by April they were struggling to mobilize enough people to participate in marches and demonstrations. Many residents wanted to take part, but the civil disobedience strategies involved getting arrested (on purpose), and many adults couldn't risk losing their jobs. That's when the idea for a Children's March came about—the young black teenagers and children of Birmingham experienced the awful effects of segregation every day, in and outside of their classrooms. They'd grown up with the movement, watching their parents get involved and even hearing Dr. King speak in their churches.

Civil rights leaders began doing outreach to local high school and college students, and they held training sessions to teach young people the basics of nonviolent civil disobedience. Many of the young people attended the trainings in secret because their parents didn't want them to be part of it; they were terrified that their children would be arrested, jailed, beaten—or worse. The students referred to the day of the march as D-Day, because it was the day they were going to ditch school to march for justice.

D-Day came on May 2, 1963. Nearly 1,000 children and teenagers from the Birmingham area headed to the 16th St. Baptist Church, with some students coming from rural schools as far as 10 miles away. They gathered in the church, went over the plan with the organizers, and waited for a local radio station to play the gospel song that would be the cue to start the march. The song came on, and the church doors opened.

Their stated goal was to march downtown to speak to the mayor of Birmingham about segregation, but they knew they'd be arrested before that actually happened. Their real goal was to fill up the jails and overwhelm the police. They walked two by two in groups of 50, singing freedom songs. When the first group got arrested and put in the paddy wagon to go to jail, another group headed out of the church and followed the same route. When that group was arrested, there was another, ready to go. By the end of the day, more than 500 elementary, middle school, high school, and college students were in jail.

The next day was referred to as Double D-Day; even more students walked out of school to attempt the march once again. This time, however, the students were met by Bull Connor, the notoriously racist public safety commissioner. He ordered the police to use violent tactics to stop the youth, including blasting them with fire hoses and letting eight vicious police dogs attack them. Some students stood bravely in the face of the fire hoses chanting "Freedom!", but the water pressure was too much for anyone to bear. Hundreds more young people were arrested, and many were injured and traumatized. Journalists captured striking photographs of black teenagers being attacked by German shepherds and blasted with fire hoses, which ended up on the front pages of newspapers around the world.

The clashes between Birmingham police and the young marchers continued for four more days. The jails were filled with high school and college students who sang songs, told stories, and comforted the youngest ones. Dr. King visited them and delivered an inspirational speech from outside the jail. In the end, more than 2,500 young people were arrested—and thousands more were inspired. Bull lost the next election, and the city council overturned its segregation policy.

CHICANO BLOWOUTS
1968

IN MARCH 1968, a group of Mexican American high school students in East Los Angeles led a series of historic walkouts and marches to protest unequal conditions in their schools. Known as the Blowouts, the events, which took place over several weeks, helped to galvanize the Chicano movement and change the conversation about public education and Latino students in California (Chicano is another term for Mexican American that became a symbol of ethnic pride in the 1960s).

During the late 1960s, education statistics for Mexican Americans in Los Angeles were grim: only one out of four Chicano students completed high school, as schools with high numbers of Chicano students were under-funded and understaffed. At Garfield High School, nearly 60 percent of the Mexican American students dropped out. Class sizes were huge, and students were often punished for speaking Spanish. White teachers generally had very low expectations for Chicano students, and attitudes toward them and their families were disrespectful at best, outright racist at worst.

As the civil rights movement swept the country, students at East Los Angeles high schools began to see that they, too, deserved better. They deserved encouragement and support. They deserved to see their cultures and histories reflected in textbooks. They deserved opportunity. They tried to talk to school officials and the school board about their concerns, but they were ignored. The only solution, they decided, was to get people's attention. They decided to stage a walkout so massive it would be more like a *blowout*.

A group of students worked for months to plan the walkouts, coordinating with students from numerous schools in the area, as well as members of the Brown Berets, a student-led activist group. There was no social media, no text messages—they had to rely on word of mouth, but they also had to keep the plan secret. On the morning of March 6, 1968, the time came. Students ran through the halls calling "Blowout! Blowout!" And that's what they did. Over 4,000 Chicano students and their supporters walked out of five East Los Angeles high schools that day. They did it again the next day, and the next. By the end of the week, over 15,000 students were marching out of 16 public high schools, demanding *justicia y educación*.

Finally, the media paid attention. Politicians did too, with one congressman showing up to support the students and asking police to leave them alone. School board members paid attention, coming to the student rallies and negotiating with student leaders over megaphones, in front of thousands of onlookers. The walkouts and marches continued for a few weeks. Students, families, teachers, and other activists formed a committee and presented a list of 39 demands to the school board.

Although the school board failed to honor all of the demands, the Blowouts did make an impact on the district. They showed that Chicano students were serious about getting quality education and were willing to take big risks to get it. The actions made an even bigger impact on the students who participated; they felt a renewed sense of pride and empowerment. Many of the organizers went on to college, and a number became community activists and educators, including Vickie Castro, who became one of the first Latinos on the Los Angeles School Board, 25 years after she helped lead the Blowouts.

ON FEBRUARY 14, 2018, a teenager armed with an automatic firearm walked onto the campus of Marjory Stoneman Douglas High School (MSD) in Parkland, Florida, and began firing his weapon. The rampage lasted six minutes, and despite training, drills, and security measures at the school, he took the lives of 17 students and staff. The massacre in Parkland occurred in mid-February, just seven weeks into the new year—but it was the sixth school shooting of 2018. By the end of the year, there would be 24, with 114 people killed or injured. The tragic event that took place at MSD was not unique in America. What *was* unique was how the students responded.

The day after the tragedy, a group of surviving students came together to cry, mourn, and support each other. They also decided to take action. They were sick of it being accepted as "normal" for students to lose their lives to gun violence in school, and they didn't want this to be just another school shooting.

They began by starting a Facebook page called #NeverAgain, as in: never again will something like this happen.

Two days after the shooting, they held a press conference on live TV, announcing the March for Our Lives, to be held just over a month later, on March 24, 2018. They demanded changes to gun laws in their state and across the country. MSD student Cameron Kasky told the cameras, "People are saying that it's not time to talk about gun control, and we can respect that. Here's a time: March 24, in every single city."

For the next month, the students, families, and community members from MSD worked to plan a march that was also a national movement. They met with politicians, leaders from major organizations, and celebrities, and did constant interviews with the media. They received support, advice, and money from many sources, but in the end, the young people organized the march. They made sure that the main event, which would take place in Washington, DC, wasn't just about them. They wanted to include young people from all over the country who've been impacted by gun violence—especially black and brown students from communities that see disproportionate rates of shootings, but whose tragic losses don't always make the news.

When the day came, hundreds of thousands of people flooded the streets to march and to listen to the powerful lineup of speakers, all of whom were kids and teenagers: no politicians, no parents, no fancy celebrities. Those supporters stayed on the sidelines and let the voice of 11-year-old Naomi Wadler ring out, as she declared, "I represent the African American women who are victims of gun violence, who are simply statistics instead of vibrant, beautiful girls full of potential."

Samantha Fuentes, an 18-year-old who survived being shot by the Parkland gunman, had the crowd sing "Happy Birthday" to her friend Nick Dworet, who did not survive. Yolanda Renee King, the nine-year-old granddaughter of Dr. Martin Luther King Jr., told the crowd, "I have a dream that enough is enough, and that this should be a gun-free world. Period." And Emma Gonzalez, who emerged as a powerful, outspoken leader in the March for Our Lives movement, demonstrated the power of silence when she stopped speaking and just stood onstage for 6 minutes and 20 seconds: the length of time it took for the shooter to complete his rampage.

And it wasn't just in Washington, DC: on March 24, 2018, there were more than 800 sister marches in other cities across the United States and around the world. Nearly two million people demonstrated on that day, committed to a world where everyone is safe from senseless gun violence.

M IS ALSO FOR . . .

MAMIE TILL-MOBLEY: The mother of Emmett Till, a 14-year-old African American boy who was violently murdered in 1955. Mamie's decision to hold an open-casket funeral for her son was seen as a catalyst for the civil rights movement.

#METOO: The movement against sexual harassment and sexual assault created by Tarana Burke in 2006 and popularized in 2017, as social media users began using the hashtag #MeToo.

MONTGOMERY BUS BOYCOTT: The social and political protests in 1955–56 against racial segregation in Montgomery, Alabama's, public transit system.

N

IS FOR
NO NUKES!

AND THE PIONEERING PEOPLE
WHO WORK FOR PEACE

"Shall we put an end to the human race; or shall mankind renounce war?"
—RUSSELL-EINSTEIN MANIFESTO, JULY 1955

IN AUGUST 1945, JUST before the end of World War II, the United States dropped two nuclear bombs on Japan: first on August 6, over the city of Hiroshima, then on August 9, over the city of Nagasaki. Together, those two bombs killed more than 200,000 people and injured hundreds of thousands more, most of them innocent civilians. They were the first and last nuclear bombs ever used in combat.

While no country has detonated a nuclear bomb during combat since then, those two terrible days forever changed the face of warfare, the centuries-long push for global peace, and the ethics of how science and technology can and should be used. The bombings ushered in what's called the atomic age, an era marked by the development of atomic energy and weaponry, as well as the Cold War, a decades-long standoff between the US and the former Soviet Union. Both powerful nations engaged in an intense arms race to see who could develop the most powerful, destructive nuclear weapons.

The bombings also launched decades of fierce resistance to nuclear weapons from people all over the world—from Catholic nuns and priests to Nobel Prize–winning physicists to suburban mothers and house-wives. Native American elders and radical anarchists came together in the Nevada desert to stop nuclear testing. Scientists, schoolchildren, and senators worked together to push for an international treaty. Young hippies and elderly grandmothers marched side by side in mass demonstrations. And community members organized to stop the construction of nuclear power plants in their home towns. Over several decades, these people used many different tactics to achieve a singular goal: an end to the development and use of weapons of mass destruction.

By the 1970s, the phrases "No nukes!" and "Ban the bomb!" were familiar rallying cries across the country, appearing on bumper stickers and buttons, protest signs and ban-ners. But the movement to eliminate nuclear weapons started earlier, in the mid-1950s, as the United States and its Soviet counterparts ramped up efforts to develop and test bigger, more powerful bombs.

MOST OF AMERICA'S NUCLEAR testing occurred in the deserts of Nevada, on sacred native land belonging to indigenous tribes like the Western Shoshone. From 1945 to 1963, the United States tested 206 nuclear weapons in the atmosphere—100 in Nevada and 106 in the South Pacific—and each released radioactive fallout: the toxic particles that get carried into the atmosphere after a nuclear explosion and fall back down to earth, being absorbed into the soil and potentially sickening—or killing—people and animals. Fallout can also be carried by the wind, meaning that the dangers of nuclear radiation aren't limited to the immediate explosion zone.

This became especially clear in 1954, when the US detonated a hydrogen bomb on Bikini Atoll, a remote chain of islands in the Pacific whose 167 indigenous inhabitants had been forcibly removed to make way for bomb testing. The bomb was 450 times more powerful than the ones dropped over Japan—to the shock and surprise of the scientists who created it. The radioactive fallout rained down on a Japanese fishing boat 90 miles away, severely poisoning 23 crew members.

Fear of nuclear war and fallout from a nuclear bomb swept the globe. In the US, schools conducted regular drills where children learned how to shelter in place in case of an attack. Some people built fallout shelters, stocking them with canned goods in case they had to live underground after an attack.

One feature of the Nevada Test Site was Survival Town, a fake American city complete with furnished homes and realistic mannequins, built by the Department of Defense to see what would survive an actual attack. The government worked to prepare Americans for a potential attack—but they also told the public that the development and testing of nuclear weapons was entirely safe.

Not everyone believed this, however. In fact, some of the most powerful opposition to nuclear proliferation (the rapid development of nuclear weapons and technologies) came from the scientific community, which saw it as science gone wrong. Nuclear development had been hailed by many as the greatest scientific achievement the world had seen. The scientists who worked on the Manhattan Project, America's top-secret effort to develop the atomic bomb, were considered geniuses. But after the bombings of Hiroshima and Nagasaki, many in the scientific community were horrified. *Do we want to use science to improve life on earth or to destroy it?* they asked. As the Cold War began to intensify, scientists worldwide began to issue dire warnings. In 1955, days before he died, Nobel Prize–winning physicist Albert Einstein signed a statement condemning nuclear proliferation, calling on world leaders to destroy all atomic weapons and end war itself.

In 1957 peace activist Ava Helen Pauling and her husband, Linus, gathered the signatures of thousands of prominent scientists for an Appeal by American Scientists to the Government and Peoples of the World. The appeal came from some of the world's most respected scientific minds. But it lacked *data.* Scientists knew that each time an atomic weapon was detonated, it released radioactive isotopes like cesium 137 and strontium 90, a cancer-causing metal with a half-life of 30 years ("half-life" is the amount of time it takes for a substance to be reduced by half; during that time, the substance is still emitting high levels of dangerous radioactivity). These substances were entirely new

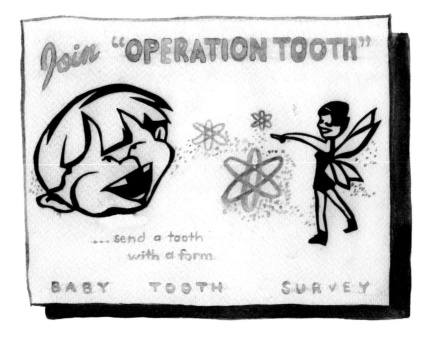

to scientists and to the environment: they didn't exist at all until nuclear weapons testing began. Scientists knew that fallout was happening, but no one knew *how much* was actually being absorbed by human bodies.

THAT'S WHAT DR. LOUISE REISS, a physician in St. Louis, Missouri, was determined to figure out. From 1959 to 1961, she led a groundbreaking study that would confirm many people's deepest fears about nuclear fallout, and would have a huge impact on President John F. Kennedy. It involved data from an unlikely source: the baby teeth of thousands of American children.

Dr. Reiss; her husband, Dr. Eric Reiss; and several other scientists and professors from local universities formed a group called the Greater St. Louis Citizens' Committee for Nuclear Information. Like many Americans, they were deeply concerned about nuclear

testing. They wanted to use the scientific method to show how radioactive fallout was impacting Americans by determining precisely how much strontium 90 was present in the bodies of young children. Because the chemical makeup of strontium 90 is similar to calcium, they knew it would be absorbed easily by teeth and bones.

Their hypothesis was that, even though the Nevada Test Site was 1,500 miles from St. Louis, the radioactive debris was getting carried east by the winds, entering the soil, and working its way up through the food chain. It got into the grass cows ate, then into the milk the cows produced, then into the babies and children who drank the fresh local milk.

Testing had already proved that milk produced by dairy cows in the St. Louis area showed the highest rates of strontium 90 of any milk tested in the entire country. If the scientists could test the bones or teeth of children, they could determine whether this radioactive material was being absorbed into their bodies. And since every young child had baby teeth that would eventually fall out, Dr. Reiss and her team launched the St. Louis Baby Tooth Survey, with the goal of collecting and testing as many teeth as possible.

But the children expected their baby teeth to go to the Tooth Fairy (who would leave them a reward), not to a laboratory, so Dr. Reiss, who had worked for years as a physician for her school district and who was the mother of a young child herself, launched a public health campaign to convince children (and their parents) to send the teeth to "science" instead of the Tooth Fairy. She wanted to make science feel exciting to children, and to make families feel like they were part of an important project. She designed a badge that read I GAVE MY TOOTH TO SCIENCE, as well as a certificate of participation. She and her volunteers visited elementary schools, churches, daycares, and dentist and pediatrician offices. They talked to the YMCA, school superintendents, local papers, and Girl and Boy Scout troops, convincing the community to participate in the study. At the height of the Cold War anxiety, when fears of war and bombs loomed large, the Tooth Survey was a way to be part of a solution.

And it worked: Dr. Reiss's team was soon collecting 750 teeth per week, often with letters from eager children, addressed to the Tooth Fairy and to "the brave scientists." Each tooth was accompanied by a card that parents filled out, providing the team with basic data. The teeth and cards were sent directly to Dr. Reiss's home; her son recalls his childhood home being filled with women sitting around card tables, sorting through stacks of envelopes and piles of teeth. Each tooth and its card were placed in a labeled envelope to be sent to the lab, where scientists ran controlled, thorough tests. The effort became so well known that the postal service knew where to deliver envelopes addressed simply "Tooth Fairy, St. Louis."

IN NOVEMBER 1961, Dr. Reiss published the initial findings in the respected journal *Science*, presenting the world with some of the first concrete data proving the widespread and dangerous effects of radioactive fallout. The results showed that levels of strontium 90 found in children's teeth were increasing every year. Children born in 1954 had four times as much strontium 90 in their teeth as those born in 1951. News of the results rippled through the scientific community, and eventually reached President Kennedy, who was in the middle of negotiating a major treaty to ban above-ground nuclear testing.

It wasn't long before Dr. Reiss's home telephone rang: it was President Kennedy, eager to discuss the findings of her research. Soon after their conversation, Dr. Reiss's husband presented more of their findings to Congress; the evidence continued to show increasing levels of strontium 90 that rose and fell in correlation with atomic bomb tests. This scientific evidence, combined with immense pressure from activists and concerned citizens, led President Kennedy to sign the historic 1963 Partial Nuclear Test Ban Treaty, which banned atomic testing underwater, in space, and in the atmosphere. It was one of the first and most powerful international environmental treaties.

Dr. Reiss and her family moved to Chicago, but the St. Louis Tooth Survey continued until 1970, ultimately collecting more than 350,000 teeth and continuing to provide powerful data about the effects of fallout on children. A second round of testing found a 50-percent drop in strontium 90 in children born in 1968, compared with those born before the treaty went into effect.

The treaty didn't make the nuclear problem go away. It banned above-ground testing of nuclear bombs, but testing continued underground. The movement for nuclear disarmament and test bans continued for the next several decades, as organizations like Women Strike for Peace, Plowshares, Peace Action, Women's International League for Peace and Freedom (WILPF), Greenpeace, the Clamshell Alliance, and many more led the resistance to nuclear proliferation and eventually to the construction of nuclear power plants. The St. Louis Tooth Survey is one of thousands of efforts that have been made to draw attention to the dangers of nuclear weapons and war, and just one example of how scientists have used data, research, and public engagement to promote a peaceful future.

N IS ALSO FOR . . .

NATIONAL PARKS: The system of federally designated and protected natural lands covering more than 80 million acres across America.

NEW NEGRO: A term associated with the Harlem Renaissance and popularized by philosopher Alain LeRoy Locke that described the attitudes of African Americans who were no longer willing to tolerate inequality and Jim Crow laws.

NINETEENTH AMENDMENT: The constitutional amendment ratified in 1920 that granted American women the right to vote in federal elections.

NOW (NATIONAL ORGANIZATION FOR WOMEN): A nonprofit organization dedicated to the fair and equal treatment of women, founded in 1966 by 49 women, including Pauli Murray, Betty Friedan, and Shirley Chisholm.

WOMEN UNITE

OUR BODIES OURSELVES

A BOOK BY AND FOR WOMEN

BY THE BOSTON WOMEN'S HEALTH BOOK COLLECTIVE

$2.95

O

IS FOR

OUR BODIES, OURSELVES

AND THE COLLECTIVE THAT WROTE THE BOOK ON WOMEN'S HEALTH

"We were excited and our excitement was powerful. We wanted to share both our excitement and what we were learning. We saw ourselves differently, and our lives began to change."

—FROM THE INTRODUCTION TO *OUR BODIES, OURSELVES*

IT HAS SOLD MORE than 4.5 million copies and been translated into 31 languages. The Library of Congress lists it as one of the books that has shaped America. It's one of the bestselling books of all time about women's health, and here's the thing: the authors weren't doctors, or medical experts, or even professional writers. They were a curious, committed, passionate group of women who believed in the power of information and education. And they changed the way that generations of women have come to understand their bodies.

In the spring of 1969, a small college in Boston held an event called the Female Liberation Conference—it may have been the first-ever feminist conference. "Women's Liberation" was the name given to the feminist movement that emerged in America during the 1960s (it was often shortened to "Women's Lib," and many now refer to it as "second-wave feminism," with the first wave being the 19th- and early 20th-century suffrage movements). As women began to question society's expectations for them, a new kind of feminist consciousness and activism emerged, led by figures like Gloria Steinem, Flo Kennedy, Dorothy Pitman Hughes, and Bella Abzug, and informed by groundbreaking books like Betty Friedan's *The Feminine Mystique.*

One of the conference workshops was "Women and the Control of Their Bodies." It was taught by Nancy Miriam Hawley, who became interested in this topic after she'd asked her doctor a simple question about the new birth control medication he'd prescribed to her. She was concerned about the possible side effects of taking hormones while breastfeeding her new baby, so she asked her doctor to explain what was actually in the pill. The doctor's response? He laughed. Then he patted her on the head and said "Don't you worry your pretty little head. Just take it." Nancy was furious—but she was also motivated to do something about it. She began questioning how women were treated by doctors, and she decided to learn about her own body.

In the 1960s, approximately 90 percent of all doctors were male, 98 percent of OB/GYNs (doctors who specialize in women's reproductive health and help provide care for women through pregnancy and delivery) were male. Women were given limited information about pregnancy and birth, and during the 1950s it was common for a pregnant woman to be strapped down to a hospital bed and sedated while giving birth. Male doctors often delivered critical health information about female patients (like whether they were pregnant, or infected with a sexually transmitted infection) to the husbands, instead of speaking directly to the women. When it came to women's bodies and health, the general attitude was that doctors know best, women know very little, and it should stay that way.

BUT THERE AT THE conference, with Nancy at the front of the room, a group of women began to change that. As they talked, their stories came pouring out. For most of them, it was the first time they'd ever talked openly about their own bodies in the company of other women. It was emotional, and powerful, and they didn't want it to end. Before the conference was over, they made a plan to meet again.

It became a weekly event: they met in each other's homes, at first calling themselves "the Doctor's Group" because their initial goal was to compile a list of good, trustworthy doctors in the area that they could share with other women. They'd all been raised to believe that doctors were the experts. But as they shared their experiences, they realized that many of them had

been doubted, or blamed for things that weren't their fault. They'd been laughed at for asking questions, or made to feel stupid. What if, instead, they could learn from each other?

The conversations quickly expanded beyond just doctors. These were well-educated women, but the more they talked, the more they realized how little information they'd been given access to. Basic anatomy, menstruation, pregnancy, childbirth, puberty, sexuality, and sexual feelings—these are all important topics that they'd never been allowed to talk or learn about. Sharing their own stories often felt exciting, though it could be a little embarrassing too. But the more they met and shared, the more comfortable they felt.

This kind of gathering was known as *consciousness raising*, or CR, and it was a big part of the women's movement in the 1960s and '70s. The idea might seem simple, but at the time its use by women was unprecedented. In a CR group, women gathered together to discuss a topic and share their own personal experiences, which helped them to better understand the impact of sexism on their lives, and their sense of self. By expressing themselves and listening to others, they became more *conscious* of the obstacles and challenges they faced due to sexism, and they realized that they were not alone in many of their experiences. CR was one of many tools that the women's movement borrowed from the civil rights movement—a number of the women were active in that movement as well and learned a lot about organizing and communicating.

THEY BEGAN TO CALL themselves the Boston Women's Health Collective (BWHC), and they came up with a summer project: research a women's health-related topic that feels most important to you, get together in small groups to discuss what you've learned, then write a paper about it. In the fall, they would present these papers as "courses" to help other women learn too.

This was thrilling—and intimidating. They weren't "experts," but did that really matter? And what *makes* someone an expert, anyway?

As they each got to work, diving deep into topics like menstruation, the stages of pregnancy, and birth control, the women realized that they *did* know a lot already. Just because they weren't doctors didn't mean they knew nothing about their own bodies. They learned equally from official sources (like textbooks, medical journals, and interviews with doctors and nurses) and from each other. It became clear that by combining scientific knowledge with personal experience they could gain a much deeper understanding of these complex issues.

One woman had a young child and had suffered postpartum depression; her mother had experienced the same thing, but there was almost no information about it in textbooks. She decided to write about that and used the experiences of her mother and herself, as well as information from a doctor. The BWHC motto soon became: "Women are the best experts on themselves."

They began to teach the courses, holding them in any space they could get, including daycare centers, churches, and homes in the Boston area. Turnout was high, as was enthusiasm—but they wanted to reach more women in other areas. They decided to take the papers and courses they'd developed and turn them into a pamphlet that could be distributed "underground"—a popular way to publish and share controversial information.

THE VERY FIRST EDITION of what would soon become *Our Bodies, Ourselves* was not exactly a *book*; it was more like a giant stack of pages stapled together. It took a year for the women to brainstorm, research, write,

edit, and type all 193 pages (this was before computers!). They raised $1,500 and printed 5,000 copies themselves. They called it *Women and Their Bodies: A Course*, and it included an introduction that stated "We are saying this: Knowledge is POWER."

The idea was that people would use it as a guide to teach their own workshops, in their own communities. It cost 75 cents, and they distributed it by hand at workshops. The demand was so high that they made a second edition, this one published by a local publisher (no more staples). They changed the book's name to *Our Bodies, Ourselves*, and the price went down to 40 cents.

Every page was packed with vital information, and chapters covered everything from nutrition to marriage to menstruation. The section on pregnancy and childbirth went over every step in the process—how babies develop and grow, how the hormones in the body change, what happens during different stages of labor and delivery. There were photographs and hand-drawn charts and illustrations. Each section included "traditional" medical information and advice alongside personal anecdotes from women about their own experiences.

The book also covered potentially controversial topics. A section about lesbian experience and identity was written by a group of gay women. There was information about masturbation and self-pleasure, as well as abortion, a medical procedure to end a pregnancy that was illegal in most US states until 1972. The authors knew that women had been seeking illegal abortions for decades and that these procedures could be dangerous—or deadly. They believed that women should be able to decide what to do with their own bodies, and the book offered honest information to help keep women safe.

Demand for the book did not let up. Orders poured in from all over the country, and within two years, they'd sold more than 250,000 copies. Stories and feedback flooded in. Many readers wrote letters about how they'd brought the book to medical appointments, challenging doctors and saying, "Look what it says here in this book. . . ." Many shared suggestions on what to include in future editions. And, the authors realized, it wasn't just women who were learning from the book. They heard from men who valued the information too, as it helped them to better understand the bodies and lives of their partners, friends, and family members.

BY 1972 A MAJOR publisher approached the BWHC and offered to print the book, which had become a massive underground success. While the members were skeptical about moving to a mainstream publisher, they knew this was their best chance to reach even more women. They negotiated an impressive contract that let them have full editorial control, meaning *they* would decide what went into the book, not the publisher (this included the cover design, which is rare for authors). The publisher agreed to translate *Our Bodies, Ourselves* into Spanish and to sell copies at a discount to women's clinics. And they agreed to a cap on the retail price, meaning the publisher couldn't raise the price above a certain amount. The BWHC wanted the book to be as accessible as possible.

And that's how it's been ever since. The BWHC has remained active for nearly 50 years, continuing to work together to educate the public about women's health.

They've published nine updated editions of *Our Bodies, Ourselves*, as well as additional books like *Ourselves, Growing Older*, which addresses the experiences of older women. Over the years they've included a diverse range of voices and perspectives and updated content about race, body image, women with disabilities, technology, and transgender and gender-nonconforming people. They have been involved in creating and advocating for better healthcare policies and inspiring new generations to carry on the work of empowering women with knowledge, confidence, and self-acceptance.

Our Bodies, Ourselves has also inspired similar projects: in 2014, a group of transgender people published *Trans Bodies, Trans Selves*, a book by and for the transgender community that offers insight, information, and guidance for trans folks navigating a medical and healthcare system that too often doesn't understand their needs, or even acknowledge their existence. In the book's afterword, the original *Our Bodies, Ourselves* founders write: "The revolutionary point is that we can name our gender identity for ourselves and rightfully expect respect and recognition. 'Our bodies, ourselves' grows in meaning daily."

O IS ALSO FOR . . .

OBERGEFELL V. HODGES: The 2015 Supreme Court case that found that the fundamental right to marry is guaranteed to same-sex couples by both the Due Process Clause and the Equal Protection Clause of the Fourteenth Amendment.

OBERLIN-WELLINGTON RESCUE: A key moment in abolitionist history when 600 black and white citizens of Oberlin and Wellington, Ohio, came together to free a formerly enslaved man from slave-catchers and get him safely to Canada.

OPEN SOURCE: A way of distributing computer software that lets users freely download the source code, and study, change, and distribute the software for any purpose. The open source model has spread beyond software to influence activism, media, and community development.

ORAL HISTORIES: An important form of historical documentation that uses interviews, storytelling, and first-person recollections to gain multiple perspectives on the histories of families, communities, and events. Oral histories are primary sources that fill in the gaps of historical accounts by providing insight and information that written sources don't.

P

IS FOR
POP ART

AND THE RADICAL CREATIONS
OF SISTER CORITA

"When art has changed, it's because the
world was changing."
—SISTER CORITA, ARTIST AND EDUCATOR

AMERICAN POP ART EMERGED in the late 1950s
as part of the post–World War II era, when
big companies increasingly used advertising
to present their products as the quickest,
easiest way to achieve a normal, happy life.
New technologies like television and magazines printed ads in color, not just black and
white, so advertisers competed to make the
most visually arresting ads possible. They
often borrowed ideas, colors, and techniques from the art world—and then pop
artists started borrowing them back, using
their art to reflect this intense focus on
consumerism.

"Pop" is short for *popular,* as in popular
culture—that is, the images and media
that most of the population tends to see
and know. Pop artists borrowed images and
phrases from popular culture, including
cartoons, comic books, advertisements,
billboards, and even packages of supermarket foods. They also borrowed the concept
of mass production from the factories that
churned out identical products and images,
and began using methods like screen
printing that allowed them to make multiple
replicas of one image, over and over.

Like nearly all art movements, pop has its
roots in movements that came before it,
like dadaism, which used absurdity to react
to the horrors of World War I, and surrealism,
which explored dreams and the subcon-
scious mind. Pop was also a response to
abstract expressionism, a style that emerged
immediately after World War II, with abstract
images created by visible brush strokes
that look messy and spontaneous. These
paintings were often oversized, and many
of the artists used lots of paint to create
varied textures on the canvas to produce
emotion rather than a representation of a
specific image.

Abstract expressionist artists like Jackson
Pollock, Alma Thomas, Helen Frankenthaler,
Mark Rothko, and Joan Mitchell helped to
established New York City as the center of
the American art scene. In contrast, pop
artists, like Roy Liechtenstein, Jasper Johns,
and Jim Dine, created bright, playful works
that featured immediately recognizable
images such as soup cans, Mickey Mouse,
Superman, Coca-Cola, and the American flag.

ONE OF THE BEST-KNOWN pop artists doing this kind of work was Andy Warhol. During the mid-1960s, Andy lived and worked in a New York studio known as the Factory. There he created all kinds of pop art: screen prints, short films, music, magazines, plays, performances, and parties. It was also a hangout for all kinds of people: fellow artists, drag queens, models, runaways, and rock stars. He called them the Warhol Superstars, and they were his factory workers, helping him assemble and produce his artworks.

During this same time period, on the other side of the country, another kind of pop art factory appeared. In a small room at a Catholic college in Los Angeles, groups of young women worked together to make art; they huddled over large pieces of paper, poured bright ink onto screens made of silk, hung up finished prints to dry, developed film in darkrooms, sketched, drew, painted, and designed.

Like the Warhol Superstars, they experimented with color, technique, form, and content. But their look was quite different from that of the wild New York crowd; most of these artists were dressed in the black-and-white habits traditionally worn by nuns. They made their own designs and prints, but they also assisted their teacher in the production of her groundbreaking work. Her name was Sister Corita, and she was a teacher, a nun, and one of the most prolific pop artists most people have never heard of.

IN 1962 SISTER CORITA was teaching at Immaculate Heart College, a Catholic school in Los Angeles that was part of the Catholic Church and the Order of the Immaculate Heart of Mary. One day, she took her students to see an art show at a small gallery. The show exhibited 32 paintings done by Andy Warhol, then an up-and-coming New York City artist whose work had never been seen on the West Coast. Each painting depicted a can of Campbell's soup, one of the most popular canned soup brands in America. Some people thought these highly realistic paintings of giant soup cans were nonsense—one newspaper mocked the show, and another local gallery displayed 32 actual cans of soup in its window as a joke.

But Sister Corita loved it. Those soup can paintings would go on to be famous works of art, and they shifted the way she thought about art. Looking at those soup cans sparked a new sense of artistic possibility and ideas about the power of using familiar, everyday things to convey her own big ideas about faith, love, and peace.

Like Andy Warhol, Sister Corita preferred the medium of serigraphy, or screen printing, which she taught herself to do in the 1950s. Serigraphy is a printing process in which a fine screen (usually made of silk) is stretched over a wooden frame. Using stencils, the artist blocks off parts of the screen and then pours ink over it. The artist spreads the ink with a squeegee, which forces the ink through the screen everywhere except where the stencils have been placed, to create shapes on the paper below. To add new colors to the print, the artist adds new screens with new stencils and pours on different colored inks. This can be repeated multiple times for multi-layered, saturated prints with many images and colors. Sister Corita loved this process of layering, and sometimes created prints with up to 23 different colors and screens.

The day after the soup cans show, Sister Corita took her students to the supermarket down the street from the convent. She told them to try and see the packaging in a new way, from the perspective of an artist, not just a consumer. She took her own advice and created a print based on the iconic Wonder Bread logo of blue, red, and yellow dots, connecting the concept of "wonder" not only to a product but also to her deep religious feelings.

SISTER CORITA WAS NO stranger to contemporary art. She was already very aware of the art world, especially of the artists pushing boundaries of form and style. She'd been teaching art since 1947, and she loved exposing her students to new ideas, taking them to galleries and museums around Los Angeles, and inviting guests like composer John Cage, director Alfred Hitchcock, and architect Buckminster Fuller to speak in her classroom. She collaborated with the designers Ray and Charles Eames and visited the studio of painter Mark Rothko.

She was also an accomplished artist already: the same year that she saw Andy Warhol's soup cans, a Los Angeles gallery exhibited her prints, and in 1963 the Whitney Museum purchased one of her pieces. Nonetheless, Andy's bold use of consumer imagery opened up a new creative path for her. She began taking images and slogans from billboards, bread wrappers, and magazine advertisements and manipulating them to make them new. She almost always incorporated additional text alongside the images, written by hand in a distinct cursive scrawl. She included song lyrics from bands like the Beatles and Jefferson Airplane; quotes from writers like E. E. Cummings, Walt Whitman, Lorraine Hansberry, and Anaïs Nin; and the words of her students and friends, like the antiwar activist priest Daniel Berrigan. She

also quoted religious texts, ranging from the Bible and the Bhagavad-Gita (the ancient Hindu sacred text) to traditional Native American prayers. The text allowed the viewer to experience the familiar brands and slogans in unexpected ways. Sister Corita felt she was doing what artists had always done: finding beauty in and working with the ideas, objects, and words around them.

SISTER CORITA WAS ALSO highly aware of the tumultuous world beyond her close-knit religious community. She wanted to make art that reflected the violence, conflict, and social unrest of the 1960s. This set her work apart from that of the other pop artists who were gaining art-world fame; their work tended to be emotionally detached. It presented aspects of American culture, but it didn't necessarily comment on it or take a political stance. Sister Corita's work was the opposite: it didn't shy away from controversy. It was emotional and passionate, and proudly declared feelings of love, faith, and peace. One of Sister Corita's prints features supermarket ads for bread and peaches, the price of 88 cents, and quotes about hunger ("the only real thing is hunger"), faith ("for us christ became bread"), and poverty (a quote from President Lyndon B. Johnson).

In 1965, a series of deadly riots broke out in the predominantly black Los Angeles neighborhood of Watts, not far from Sister Corita's college. The National Guard was called in, and for several days the neighborhood was like a war zone. Sister Corita was outraged at the brutal treatment of African Americans in Watts and across the nation, so she created a print that combines the headline from the front page of the *Los Angeles Times* ("Eight Men Slain") with a quote from Maurice Ouellet, a white priest from Alabama who had been kicked out of the church for supporting Dr. Martin Luther King Jr. and civil rights activists in Selma, Alabama. The quote was set against a swath of red ink, which makes the newspaper look blood-stained. By including the quote from Ouellet, who got in trouble for his outspoken activism, Sister Corita may have been anticipating what would soon happen to her.

AS THE VIETNAM WAR escalated abroad, and the antiwar and civil rights movements intensified around the US, her art became more and more political. Her prints condemned the war and suggested that Christians like herself have a moral obligation to work toward justice for all humans. She created prints after the assassinations of Dr. King and Senator Robert Kennedy; the latter juxtaposed the slain leader with Jesus. This did not please the archbishop of Los Angeles, who wrote a series of letters to Immaculate Heart. Sister Corita's work, he declared, was "weird and sinister." Officials from the Catholic Church began to show up unannounced to inspect Sister Corita's art. Her colleagues defended her work, but the pressure continued, and the heads of the church wanted Sister Corita to stop making provocative political art.

Between 1962 and 1968, Sister Corita made more than 300 prints that drew from—and expanded—the pop art aesthetic. Like the big names of the contemporary art movement, she took her inspiration from consumer products and popular advertising. She used color, text, and image manipulation to turn everyday phrases into provocative artworks. Her work was playful and clever, but it was also social commentary. By connecting pop art to the social unrest of the decade, Sister Corita created something

entirely new. In 1966, the *Los Angeles Times* named her one of nine Women of the Year, and in 1967, she was on the cover of *Newsweek* magazine. But she was never considered one of the major pop artists; by the end of the 1960s, there were several major retrospectives of the "most important" pop artists of the decade, and none of them included her.

In 1968, Sister Corita left her teaching job, and moved east to Boston. In 1971, when she painted the "Rainbow Swash" on a massive gas tank near a freeway, she created the world's largest copyrighted work of art and one of Boston's most iconic landmarks. In 1985, she created the well-known LOVE stamp for the U.S. Postal Service, summing up her message with the single word written beneath bright swaths of color.

Corita Kent was a woman, a teacher, and a nun—three attributes not usually associated with successful, famous artists. She created hundreds of innovative prints in her lifetime, and her work is now held by America's most respected museums—and finally included in retrospectives and exhibits about pop art, one of the 20th century's most distinctive modern art movements.

P IS ALSO FOR . . .

PLANNED PARENTHOOD: A nonprofit organization, founded in 1965, that provides reproductive health care and family planning to millions of people each year.

PLOWSHARES: An anti–nuclear weapons pacifist movement, founded in the 1980s by the Berrigan brothers, that advocates active resistance to war.

POOR PEOPLE'S CAMPAIGN: The 1968 march on Washington, DC, planned by Dr. Martin Luther King Jr. (and led by Ralph Abernathy after Dr. King's murder) to obtain economic justice for poor people in the US.

PUBLIC EDUCATION: The system of primary and secondary schools that is free, open to all, and funded by taxes and federal money.

PUEBLO REVOLT: The 1680 uprising of indigenous Pueblo people against Spanish colonizers in present-day New Mexico.

KEITH HARING

Another American artist who used pop art to make powerful social and political work was Keith Haring. His iconic paintings and drawings were influenced by popular culture and the graffiti and street art of New York City in the late 1970s and '80s.

In 1980 Keith began doing chalk drawings in the New York subways, sometimes creating up to 40 subway drawings a day. He was committed to breaking down the barriers between public street art and the private art world of fancy galleries and museums.

Keith's use of bright colors and simple shapes (stick figures, hearts, dogs) made his work visually accessible to a wide range of people. Many of his pieces looked deceptively fun and simple but actually addressed complex, serious topics including the AIDS epidemic, South African apartheid, drug addiction, and gender and sexual identity. Like Corita Kent, he believed art was for everyone and should be as visible and widely available as possible.

Keith's career was brief but impactful. He was diagnosed with AIDS in 1988, and died of AIDS-related complications in 1990. He devoted the last few years of his life to speaking publicly about AIDS and making art to raise money for organizations that supported adults and children living with HIV and AIDS.

IGNORANCE = FEAR

SILENCE = DEATH ▲

Q

IS FOR

QUILTS

THE CRAFT THAT
CAPTURES HISTORY

WHEN YOU WRAP UP in a warm quilt to watch TV or read a book, you might not feel like you're cozying up with a historical document. But quilts have been part of American culture—documenting families and communities, war and patriotism, and the struggles for peace and equality—for centuries.

The earliest American quilts were basic and functional. But as styles, methods, and materials evolved, quilts took on special meanings, becoming both functional and decorative. They commemorated major life occasions: crib quilts welcomed new babies, wedding quilts were gifted to newlyweds. Family quilts decorated with names and

family trees became precious heirlooms and were passed down, along with the skill of quilt-making itself, from generation to generation. It wasn't long before women began using quilts as a kind of diary, recording not just family events, but national and local ones as well.

At a time when women were rarely allowed at political meetings or discussions, quilting circles became spaces for them to share opinions they couldn't express elsewhere. Many of the earliest meetings of abolitionists, temperance activists, and suffragists began in quilting and sewing circles.

While quilts can cover our beds and keep us warm, they can also tell our stories and keep us connected to our families, ancestors, and heritage. Some are displayed on museum walls as valuable art; others lie deep in trunks in the attic, waiting to be discovered. Quilts remind us of who we've been and what we can be. And as the following stories show, they can connect us to our histories, stitching together personal experience and the broader issues of the times.

ATHENS, GEORGIA
1886

FOR THE VERY FIRST TIME, Harriet Powers went to a local fair to put one of her quilts on display. Harriet was a formerly enslaved mother of nine who lived with her family on a small plot of farmland. Like many women in her community, she was a gifted quilter. At the Athens Cotton Fair, she displayed her Bible Quilt: it tells the story of the Bible in 11 panels featuring humans, animals, and celestial designs. There are Adam and Eve, with a large striped snake sneaking up on Eve. There is Jacob climbing the ladder to escape from slavery. There are the animals of Noah's ark; there is the Last Supper. The quilt has 299 individual pieces, and broken vertical stripes of cloth separate the 11 panels. This is a technique that often appears in West African textiles, and it reflects the ways that enslaved Africans passed down artistic and cultural traditions during and after the transatlantic slave trade.

A white art teacher named Jennie saw the quilt at the fair and was stunned; she later wrote in her diary that she had never seen a quilt like it. She offered to purchase it, but Harriet said no. Several years later, when Harriet and her family had fallen on hard times, she sold the quilt to Jennie for $5. Before Harriet left, she explained each panel in detail, and Jennie wrote it all down. Harriet created at least five more quilts in her life, but only the Bible Quilt and one other are known to still exist—they hang in the Smithsonian Museum and Boston Museum of Fine Arts, where they're recognized as some of the finest examples of quilting from the American South.

QUEEN LILI'UOKALANI SAT ALONE, imprisoned in her own royal palace. After struggling for several years to keep the kingdom of Hawaii from being overthrown by American businessmen, the proud leader surrendered peacefully, sacrificing her throne and her kingdom to avoid violent conflict. She had been falsely accused and convicted of treason and placed under house arrest. Armed guards stood watch while she remained inside. A lifelong songwriter, poet, and storyteller, Lili'uokalani was determined to tell her story. She gathered pieces of velvet, linen, silk, and ribbon and began, sewing these words into a square of fabric: "Imprisoned at Iolani Palace . . . We began the quilt here." She added the royal coat of arms framed by pairs of crossed Hawaiian flags. This became the center square of the Queen's Quilt, a 97 by 95-inch, 9-block quilt that tells the story of her imprisonment and the history of Hawaii.

Every piece was hand-stitched with colorful threads, and the queen used complex stitching techniques. She embroidered the names of important figures in Hawaiian history, as well as meaningful dates: the day she was forced to step down, the date of the failed revolution that led to her arrest. She created patriotic ribbons and badges and included native Hawaiian flora and fauna. During the eight long months that she was held captive in her palace, she designed, stitched, and pieced it together. It is how she passed her time, and it is how she told her story. The quilt is still there, displayed in her palace, helping to preserve and tell the history of Hawaii to visitors and native Hawaiians alike.

FATHER FRANCIS WALTER, an Episcopal priest and civil rights activist, was driving through rural Alabama, documenting cases of harassment against black families. The Selma-to-Montgomery marches had taken place just months before, not that far away, and racial tensions in the area were serious.

He drove past a wooden shack and noticed something that made him stop: hanging from a clothesline were three stunning patchwork quilts, unlike any he'd ever seen. They were brightly colored, with bold, wild geometric patterns like the contemporary paintings he'd seen in fancy New York City museums. A woman on the property ran into the woods when she saw the strange white man approaching. Father Walter understood, and he left—but he couldn't shake the beauty of those quilts.

He later returned to the home with Ella Saulsbury, a local black organizer. They told Ora McDaniels, the woman who'd run into the woods, that they'd like to buy her quilts for $10 each (twice the going rate) and then auction them off in New York City. All the money would be donated to the local civil rights organizations. Ora agreed, as did many other local quilters—the average annual income for black families in the area was less than $1,000.

Soon Father Walter met with the quilters from nearby Gee's Bend, a tiny, isolated all-black community almost completely cut off from the rest of society. (Limited ferry service to Gee's Bend was canceled by local officials when residents began traveling to nearby towns to register to vote.) In Gee's Bend, Father Walter encountered a vast, vibrant multigenerational quilting community of women who'd been creating original patterns and designs for decades, using whatever materials they could find—old overalls, worn worksheets, empty grain sacks.

Led by experienced quilter Minder Coleman (who'd once woven drapes for President Roosevelt's White House when Gee's Bend was established by the Farm Security Administration in the 1930s), the women formed a collective: the Freedom Quilting Bee. Their quilts began selling at auctions in New York City and around the country, and they caught the eye of famous artists.

The women earned enough money to support their families, to purchase a workspace with new sewing equipment, *and* to support the local civil rights organizations. They continued to work together for decades, creating original designs for big companies like Sears and helping to revive national interest in quilting and American folk art. Meanwhile, the quilts of Gee's Bend became recognized as "some of the most miraculous works of art America has produced" when they were exhibited at the Whitney Museum in New York City.

1985
SAN FRANCISCO, CALIFORNIA

EVERY YEAR SINCE 1978, Cleve Jones had organized a candlelight vigil to commemorate the life of Harvey Milk, America's first openly gay American politician. By 1985, though, Harvey's memory was not the only thing on the minds of San Francisco's gay community: they were being ravaged by a new disease. It was called AIDS, and it was terrifying; they didn't know how to stop it or why it was happening, but it had taken at least 500 men in San Francisco alone, and nearly 6,000 people nationwide. The community felt ignored

by politicians and shunned by the general public. President Ronald Reagan hadn't even said the word "AIDS" yet.

Cleve wanted to wake people up. He asked the crowd at the vigil to write the name of someone they knew who had died of AIDS on a piece of paper. They held these high and marched to San Francisco's federal building, where they taped the names all over the walls. It made Cleve think of a quilt, the kind his grandmother used to make. It gave him an idea of how he might honor the dead—many of whom didn't get funerals or gravestones because their families rejected them out of shame and fear—and make the public pay attention.

Cleve and his friends began sewing quilt panels, one for each of their 40 friends who'd died. The panels were three by six feet (the size of a grave), with eight panels to a section. They called it the NAMES Project, and they spread the word, inviting family and friends who'd lost loved ones to contribute panels. Volunteers stepped up, tirelessly collecting, organizing, and sewing the panels as they came in.

In October 1987, Cleve and his friends took 2,000 panels to Washington, DC, and laid them out on the National Mall during the National March on Washington for Lesbian and Gay Rights. The quilt was bigger than a football field—a sea of names, colors, fabrics, textures, and memories.

The panels (which are still being added) are each as unique as the lives they represent: some use traditional quilting styles, some are simple, some are wild—there are feathers and sequins and rhinestones. Many incorporate personal belongings, like scraps of favorite jeans, pieces of leather jackets, uniforms, ribbons and awards, and wedding rings.

Half a million people came to see the quilt that weekend, and the response was overwhelming. Cleve gave a speech, telling the crowd: "We bring a quilt. We hope it will help people to remember. We hope it will teach our leaders to act." The panels kept coming in, so they took the quilt on a nationwide tour, adding panels in each city. It grew to 6,000 panels, then 10,000. It became a symbol of the human toll of the AIDS epidemic, and in 1989, the quilt was nominated for the Nobel Peace Prize. Several decades later, the AIDS Memorial quilt still endures, weighing 54 tons, with 49,000 panels on 5,956 blocks—if you spend one minute looking at each panel, it will take you more than a month to view it all. It is the largest community art project in the world.

Q IS ALSO FOR . . .

QUAKERS: A historically Christian group of religious movements with a strong commitment to peace and the abolition of slavery.

QUEER: The "Q" in LGBTQ, "queer" was once a derogatory term for gay people, but has been reclaimed and is now used by many as a positive way to define and describe their non-heterosexuality.

R

IS FOR
RIOT GRRRL

AND THE REBELS WHO TOOK PUNK ROCK INTO THEIR OWN HANDS

"BECAUSE us girls crave records and books and fanzines that speak to US that WE feel included in and can understand in our own ways.

"BECAUSE we wanna make it easier for girls to see/hear each other's work so that we can share strategies and criticize-applaud each other.

"BECAUSE we want and need to encourage and be encouraged in the face of all our own insecurities.

"BECAUSE we don't wanna assimilate to someone else's (boy) standards of what is or isn't.

"BECAUSE we are angry at a society that tells us Girl = Dumb, Girl = Bad, Girl = Weak.

"BECAUSE I believe with my wholeheartmindbody that girls constitute a revolutionary soul force that can, and will, change the world for real . . . "

—FROM "RIOT GRRRL MANIFESTO" BY KATHLEEN HANNA, PUBLISHED IN 1991 IN *BIKINI KILL #2*

RIOT GRRRL WAS A genre of feminist punk music and a grassroots do-it-yourself political and cultural movement in America from around 1990 to 1996. Riot Grrrl can be hard to define—and that's intentional. As Kathleen Hanna, lead singer of the band Bikini Kill and an integral part of the Riot Grrrl movement, has said, the thing about Riot Grrrl "was that you *couldn't* define it: each person defined it as it happened." It encouraged teenagers and young women to create their own culture by teaching themselves to play guitar, start bands, make art, share ideas, and define their own existences in whatever way made sense. Riot Grrrl revived the ideas behind the feminist consciousness–raising groups of the 1970s (see page 93)—but with a punk rock twist.

IN THE EARLY 1990s in the Pacific Northwest cities of Olympia and Seattle, Washington, a new music scene was brewing. While bands like Nirvana and Pearl Jam were defining a new sound called "grunge," there was another movement happening, powered by teenage girls and young women who wanted to rock, but felt alienated, intimidated, and even unsafe in the male-dominated punk spaces.

They wanted to push to the front of a crowd and thrash their bodies to the wailing guitars. They wanted to dive off the stage and crowd surf. And they wanted to be onstage, screaming into the mic, kicking over amps, and bashing away on the drums. But they didn't feel like they could. They felt ignored by society, which didn't value the intelligence and potential of young women, and they felt dismissed by the guys in the punk scene, who saw them as potential girlfriends—not potential bandmates. So they decided to do something about it.

Tobi Vail and Kathleen Hanna were friends who shared a love for punk—and for politics. They'd read books by Audre Lorde, bell hooks, Angela Davis, and Gloria Steinem, and were well versed in feminist ideas. They were also sick of reading articles that proclaimed the feminist movement to be over. Sometimes it felt to them like the 1980s had swallowed up all the powerful progress that women had made: reproductive rights were under siege, and news stories about violent attacks on women seemed to air constantly.

Tobi had been playing drums since she was 12, and Kathleen had taught herself to play guitar. They called their band Bikini Kill, and they committed themselves to inspiring as many girls and women as possible to start their own bands. When any girl told them "I love your band!" their response was always, "Cool! Why don't you start your own? That's what we did!"

THE TERM "RIOT GRRRL" was coined after Jen Smith, a punk from Washington, DC, wrote Kathleen a letter that said something like, "This summer's gonna be a girl riot!" No one remembers *exactly* what the letter said, but the phrase stuck in Tobi's and Kathleen's heads, and a few months later they started a zine called *Riot Grrrl.* Changing the spelling of *girl* to *grrrl* felt fun and tough; it sounded like a wild animal snarling. It also felt like a way to take back the word *girl*—being female was nothing to be ashamed of, but they often felt like it was, and that feeling was often confirmed by society.

Bikini Kill soon connected with women in other cities, especially in Washington, DC, which had a thriving punk scene. A few of Tobi and Kathleen's new friends were inspired to start their own bands, and soon Bratmobile and Heavens to Betsy were playing shows too. The bands' lyrics were intense, fearless, raw—and empowering. They addressed topics like eating disorders, sexual assault, and society's unfair beauty standards—things that weren't usually part of mainstream pop music *or* underground punk songs.

AS THE RIOT GRRRL movement spread, more girls taught themselves to play instruments, wrote songs, and formed bands—like Huggy Bear, Excuse 17, and Sleater-Kinney. They made their own zines, small books stapled together and duplicated on copy machines—like *Girl Germs*, *I Heart Amy Carter*, *Jigsaw*, and *GUNK!*—which they handed out at shows or mailed across the country.

For several years, Riot Grrrl was everywhere: in the bands, in the zines, in the punk rock scene, and in the meetings and at the conventions where people gathered to talk honestly about what it meant to be a girl in America and the world. It lived in live shows, where singers would call out "Girls to the front!"—insisting that the guys move to the back so the women could occupy the space that was traditionally packed with aggressive, thrashing punk guys.

It also lived in the private correspondence of thousands of young women (and many men) who exchanged letters, mixtapes, records, postcards, and videocassettes, finding community and connection in a pre-internet world. And while the moment may have passed, making way for new subcultures and radical feminist movements, Riot Grrrl lives on in the memories of those who experienced it firsthand:

"I went to my first Riot Grrrl show at the North Shore Surf Club in Olympia in 1991. I was 18 and in my first year of college. I had already met Allison [Wolfe] and Molly [Neuman] from Bratmobile, and I had heard a lot about Bikini Kill around town. I was curious. I had grown up with liberal values and had read some feminist authors in high school, but their content seemed removed from my own personal teenage girl experience. The show was lightly attended; a lot of people stood at the sides of the room with their arms folded. Both bands were still learning how to play their instruments to some degree but gave amazing performances. Allison sang the song "Girl Germs" and did the splits on stage. Kathleen Hanna sang "Feels Blind" and I felt like I was struck by lightning. These young women were taking their own experiences with sexism, sexual assault, and harassment and making them into music! They were taking feminist ideas out of the academic world and into the universal language of music, of punk. I knew that night that I wanted to be a part of Riot Grrrl. I wanted a chance to tell my story, too."

—CORIN TUCKER, LEAD SINGER OF HEAVENS TO BETSY AND SLEATER-KINNEY

"I was part of the Olympia, Washington, community that eventually became Riot Grrrl, but a real turning point for me was seeing the band Team Dresch in New York City in 1994. They were doing a self-defense demonstration as part of their show. I'd seen other Riot Grrrl bands, but this was so different—they were all queer. It was affirming. It was a paradigm shift. My intro to the punk scene was in the Northeast, where it was more male dominated. I'd been harassed and queer-bashed, often outside of clubs after punk shows. So seeing people in my community showing me not just how to take up space, but how to *own* the space and protect myself, was incredible.

"I made a zine called 'I Heart Amy Carter,' which was about queer visibility and being from a working-class background. It was a way to connect, to find other women and gay men in the punk and Riot Grrrl scenes who'd grown up very poor like I had, who knew what it was like to be on welfare, in a family where people didn't go to high school or have jobs. This was the way to connect, to tell my story and hear others. This was before email, social media, cell phones—I told my stories in my zine, and people wrote me letters. I found a tribe within the tribe."

—TAMMY RAE CARLAND, ARTIST AND EDUCATOR

"Even though I barely knew how to play my guitar, I wanted to be in a band. After a few practices with new friends, we played a show. It was 1991 and I was so terrified that I spent the whole time with my head leaned over my guitar. I wasn't that good. I made mistakes. But my friends made me feel like the music we made was excellent and important. That made me feel great."

—JEN SMITH, MUSICIAN, ON THE FIRST TIME SHE PLAYED WITH BRATMOBILE

"The first time I encountered Riot Grrrl was 1991 when I was 17 years old. At Gilman in Berkeley a sign hung on the wall: NO RACISM, NO SEXISM, NO HOMOPHOBIA. Goals. Punk was already a big part of my life and there I saw the stage occupied by women and queer people. First Tribe 8 came on, and after that Bikini Kill. At the end of the set Kathleen Hanna announced: 'Any girls who play or want to play instruments, let's meet outside.' Five of us went out there, and she told us about Riot Grrrl: the dream that girls everywhere could learn to play instruments, start bands, make zines, and make scenes. I felt incredibly awkward and shy, but I scrawled my address on a piece of paper she passed around.

A month later a package arrived in the mail with a record and a stack of zines and a letter from Kathleen. The zines and lyrics had stories about being queer, about surviving childhood abuse—things that I didn't have language for yet. I still have the second letter she sent a couple months later: 'Hey Daniela, did you get the last package I sent you? I didn't hear back from you. How are you doing? Did you start a band? Xo Kathleen.' This was punk rock feminism! Her letter changed my life.

By the next year I was playing in the band The Gr'ups, and touring the US and Europe as an out queer person."

—DANIELA SEA, ACTOR, ARTIST, AND MUSICIAN

"In the summer of 1994, I went searching for salvation from my suburban high school nightmare. Sassy [magazine]'s Cute Band Alert and friendly record store staff eventually led me to purchase my first record, "The Real Janelle" by Bratmobile. A cool punk girl from my neighborhood spotted the record through my bag and asked me about it. I was thrilled to be called out, like I had just unlocked the door to a secret society. There were other girls like me. I would go to the record store every week looking for new releases, which is how I discovered Heavens to Betsy. It felt dangerous to listen to these songs. It felt like I could finally be free if I just belted out "I'm out of my head / I'm out of my mind" a little louder. Corin Tucker's raw anger pierced through every fiber of my being. It seems so innocent now, but just like the consciousness-raising groups of the second-wave feminist movement, Riot Grrrl changed my whole life."

—BRIDIE LEE, WRITER

"I often hear from young women who are doing research on Riot Grrrl, and they always ask, "How can I make Riot Grrrl happen again?" The thing is, Riot Grrrl was a collective response to a particular moment in time, pushed forward by a particular community of people. It can't be re-created, but it can teach us a lot. Recognize that you're going to have to make something new that's right for right now—and you have to find other people to make it with. You can do that online, but you also need to take up real-world space, make real noise, make actual sound, and work to be together and hear each other. Then you can make something new that no one's ever seen before."

—SARA MARCUS, AUTHOR OF *GIRLS TO THE FRONT: THE TRUE STORY OF THE RIOT GRRRL REVOLUTION*

R IS ALSO FOR . . .

RECONSTRUCTION: The tumultuous, transformative decades after the Civil War, when America attempted to rebuild itself, and millions of formerly enslaved Americans sought their rightful place as free and full citizens.

REDSTOCKINGS: A radical feminist group founded in 1969; the name is a reference to the phrase "bluestockings," a derogatory European slang term for female intellectuals.

#RESIST: The hashtag popularized in the wake of the 2016 election, referring to progressive resistance to the new administration.

ROE V. WADE: The 1973 Supreme Court decision that affirms the constitutional right to privacy and access to safe, legal abortions.

ROSIE THE RIVETER: A cultural icon that represented the mostly white American women who entered the workforce in shipyards and factories during World War II.

S

IS FOR
STONEWALL

AND THE NIGHT THAT CHANGED THE LGBTQ COMMUNITY FOREVER

WHEN THE NEW YORK City Police Department (NYPD) showed up to raid the Stonewall Inn in June 1969, the officers figured it would be like other raids they'd done on gay bars in the area: Open the door, turn on the lights, shut off the music. If the bar was run by the mafia, which they pretty much all were, collect bribe money from the bartender. Ask everyone for identification, then begin arresting people: the underage kids, the men holding hands, and anyone violating the "three-item rule" (an old law that required a person to wear at least three items of clothing matching their assigned gender). Kick everyone else out, and move on to the next spot. The police in New York City were used to raiding bars and arresting gay men and women;

what they weren't used to was those people fighting back.

In 1969 homosexuality was illegal in every state in America except Illinois. There were no openly gay politicians, no "out" gay celebrities. Gay and lesbian people absolutely existed, but the vast majority kept that truth hidden. There were no laws to protect gay men and women from discrimination: being gay could get you fired, evicted, arrested, beaten up—or worse. Underground organizations distributed pamphlets listing secret bars and nightclubs, usually hidden away on side streets, where gays and lesbians could gather discreetly and hopefully safely. One spot in the pamphlets was the Stonewall Inn, a run-down bar in Manhattan's Greenwich Village neighborhood.

The Stonewall was dark, dingy, and kind of smelly. But that didn't matter to the regulars who frequented it. It was a safe space where they could meet, laugh, and talk. With two dance floors, people could show off their fabulous moves, and same-gender couples could slow dance in peace.

Stonewall was known as a place that accepted *all* the queers (at the time, "queer" was an anti-gay slur that many LGBTQ people have since reclaimed and use among themselves), including the ones who weren't always welcome at "nicer" gay bars that catered to middle-class, mostly white, men. Whether you were black, Puerto Rican, or white; young or old; butch, femme, or trans; you could have fun and dance at Stonewall. It was popular with drag queens (known then as "transvestites"), transsexuals (what we now call "transgender people"), and "queens" (gender-nonconforming gay men). Many regulars were runaways who lived on the streets;

they'd been rejected by their families and had come to New York seeking acceptance. For many of the most marginalized people in the city, Stonewall offered connection and community.

ON THE NIGHT OF the Stonewall raid, the air was thick with New York City's notorious summer heat. Just after 1 a.m., eight officers from the NYPD's public morals division entered the inn. At first, it proceeded like a standard raid: the lights went up, the music stopped, and the police began to line up the 200 or so people inside, including the employees.

It's impossible to pinpoint exactly why the mood inside Stonewall began to shift, why *this* raid ended up so differently from all the others. People who were there that night recall a "feeling" in the air as people began to speak up and resist. "This isn't right," some declared, while others loudly announced "I'm not showing you my ID!" Then the police separated the transvestites from the rest of the group and tried to make them go into the restrooms to be "examined"—police wanted to check their private body parts to see if they "matched" their clothing. The transvestites said no and refused to enter the bathrooms; the tensions increased even more.

Outside Stonewall, the paddy wagon arrived, ready to take people to jail. Police began dragging people out of Stonewall and into the wagon—often with force. A crowd gathered to watch. Local residents came down from their apartments, and street kids walked over from nearby Christopher Park to see what was going on. Voices began to cry out: "Don't treat her like that!" "Leave them alone!"

At that point, many of the young people being arrested began to exhibit a sense of humor

often referred to as "camp"—some blew kisses to the crowd before being handcuffed, while others called out to the onlookers with sarcastic, silly remarks. "Where *is* my wife?" cried one queen in full drag. "I *told* her not to go far!" This kind of humor was both entertainment and a defense mechanism to cover the pain and humiliation of being arrested and harassed. Many eyewitnesses agree that the humor among the Stonewall patrons and the growing crowd of onlookers kept the mood light, at least for a while.

Officers continued to take people out of the inn, sometimes pushing and kicking those who refused to go quietly. One officer shoved a transvestite, and she turned around and hit him with her purse. He retaliated with a blow from his nightstick, and the crowd erupted. Some called for the paddy wagon to be tipped over, and they began to push on it. Others began to throw pennies and other items from their pockets. The crowd now numbered in the hundreds, and the paddy wagon was full.

MOST EYEWITNESS ACCOUNTS agree that the next turning point was the arrest of a lesbian woman who incited the crowd to take action. It was likely Stormé DeLarverie, a well-known butch lesbian drag king and nightclub performer. She began resisting when officers inside the bar grabbed her roughly, and began to push her out the door. As they attempted to force her into a patrol car, she asked them to loosen her handcuffs. When an officer hit her in the head, she turned to the swelling crowd who stood there watching and screamed: "Why don't you guys *do* something?"

One reporter on the scene later wrote: "It was at that moment that the scene became explosive." Someone threw a brick. Someone threw a bottle. Then another brick. And another bottle. Which person threw which object first is a subject of debate among some Stonewall veterans, scholars, and members of the LGBTQ community who want to know exactly what happened that night. Others argue that it doesn't matter who threw the first brick; they accept that we'll never know. Stonewall is less about the action of *one* person and more about how a community rose up.

Once the crowd became aggressive, the police retreated into the inn. They locked the doors, barricaded the windows, and called for more backup. Many of the original patrons who hadn't yet been released were still in there. The police were outnumbered, and they realized that the crowd was *not* going to go away quietly. These young, angry gay people were going to *fight*. Outside, the crowd realized their temporary victory—the police had retreated! But now they were locked inside the bar—*their* bar! *Their* Stonewall!

THE AIR FILLED WITH flying bottles, rocks, cans, and more bricks from a nearby construction site. People heaved trashcans at the windows, trying to break in to reclaim the space they'd been forced out of. A window on the second floor shattered. Someone shoved burning paper inside a glass bottle and threw it at the building; another set a piece of wood on fire and threw that. At some point, a group of men pulled a parking meter out of the ground and used it as a battering ram, trying to break down the front door.

Chants of "Gay power!," "Liberate the bar!," and "We want freedom!" filled the air. Inside, police scrambled to secure the doors and windows. At one point they located a fire hose and attempted to spray the crowd outside to get them to disperse—but the water pressure was weak, and a number of queens skipped through the water playfully, laughing at the failed attempt. It wasn't long before the side of the building was on fire. Then came the sound of sirens. The fire department arrived—along with five buses containing the riot police.

By this point the streets outside the Stonewall Inn were out of control. The cops, wearing helmets and holding large shields, attempted to clear the streets, but the crowds wouldn't back down. For hours they played a kind of cat-and-mouse game, running away from the riot police down one street, then dashing around the corner and coming up behind them on another. At one point a line of police confronted a line of young men: the police stood with their clubs drawn and their riot helmets on. The men rolled up their pant legs, put their arms around each other, and formed a kick line. Then they danced with glee in the style of the world-famous Rockettes. It infuriated the police, who rushed the dancing men and arrested them.

THE NEXT MORNING THE streets around the Stonewall Inn glittered with broken glass and debris. Between the police raid and the crowd assault, the bar itself sustained heavy damage. The uprising was covered in the *New York Times* and the *New York Post*, and while the articles were condescending and filled with insulting anti-gay language, they spread the word about what had happened. A group of activists made 5,000 copies of a flyer calling for an end to both police harassment *and* mafia control of gay bars—it was a hint of the political organizing to come.

All day long, curious people streamed to the Village to survey the scene, and that evening, Stonewall opened for business. The jukebox had been destroyed, so a sound system was brought in. It was like a block party, with 2,000 people in the streets and the bar packed wall to wall. The riot police came back, too, and tempers flared again. While many who were there say the second night was more rage-filled than the first, they also remark on how free and liberated the gay community seemed. Men embraced openly on the streets, holding hands as they ran from police. At one point, someone went to the local police precinct and slapped bright-colored bumper stickers proclaiming EQUALITY FOR HOMOSEXUALS on the parked police cars.

WHILE ALL KINDS OF people took part in the multiday events in and around Stonewall, the majority of the people on the front lines of the intense back-and-forth with police were the "queens"—the "feminine" men and trans women who'd been bullied and beaten, called names like "sissy," "limp-wrist," "fairy," and much worse. Many of them were black and Latinx street hustlers who were all too used to harassment—for trans women like Marsha P. Johnson, Sylvia Rivera, and Miss Major Griffin-Gracy, the chance to finally fight back was exhilarating.

The unrest simmered for several more days, but by late Wednesday the streets had finally quieted. There was a sense that "it" was over. Countless people were arrested and injured, including at least one officer who was seriously injured by a flying glass bottle. Remarkably, no one was killed.

In the days, weeks, and months that followed Stonewall, a stronger, more focused gay rights movement took shape. A group of activists founded the Gay Liberation Front (GLF), which created the first LGBTQ community center. Marsha P. Johnson and Sylvia Rivera formed a group known as STAR (Street Transvestite Action Revolutionaries), which focused on doing outreach to young homeless LGBTQ people, and a group of lesbian feminists formed the Lavender Menace.

On the one-year anniversary of Stonewall, the GLF held the world's first gay pride march. One of the main organizers was a woman named Brenda Howard, who's often referred to as the "Mother of Pride." They proclaimed June 28 to be Christopher Street Liberation Day, and hundreds of gay, lesbian, trans, and bisexual people marched 51 blocks from Stonewall to Central Park. The march was peaceful, with no interference from police—and overwhelming support from the onlookers who watched the unprecedented display of public, joyful pride. There are now thousands of gay pride parades around the world every year.

S IS ALSO FOR . . .

SELMA TO MONTGOMERY MARCH: The series of three civil rights protest marches along the 54-mile highway from Selma to Montgomery, Alabama, in 1965.

SILENT SPRING: A landmark book published in 1962 by scientist Rachel Carson that documents the harmful impact of pesticides on humans and the environment.

SNCC (STUDENT NONVIOLENT COORDINATING COMMITTEE): A key civil rights organization founded in 1960 and led by activists like Ella Baker, Julian Bond, Diane Nash, and Bob Moses.

Stonewall was a major moment in LGBTQ history—but it wasn't the first time the community stood up and fought back. Here are just a few milestone events that came before.

1924 Henry Gerber founded the Society for Human Rights, the US's first gay rights organization; it quickly disbanded due to harassment.

1950 Harry Hay founded the Mattachine Society, which aimed to "eliminate discrimination, derision, prejudice, and bigotry."

1955 Del Martin and Phyllis Lyon founded the Daughters of Bilitis, the first lesbian social and political organization.

1958 *One, Inc. v. Olesen*, the first Supreme Court ruling on LGBTQ rights, found that books, magazines, and newsletters with homosexual content were not automatically obscene.

1961 José Sarria, a beloved San Francisco drag queen performer, became the first openly gay person to run for office. He got nearly 8,000 votes—coming in 9th out of 30 candidates for city supervisor—and paved the way for Harvey Milk, California's first openly gay elected official in 1977.

1964 On September 19, ten people marched in front of New York City's Whitehall Military Induction Center to protest the military's discrimination against gay and lesbian people (the period after World War II, when more than 5,000 suspected gays and lesbians were kicked out of the military, was known as the "lavender scare").

1965 In Philadelphia, Pennsylvania, a popular burger joint called Dewey's had become a gathering spot for gay and gender-variant teenagers. When the management at one location told staff to refuse service to anyone who even *looked* gay, a group of teens organized a series of lunch counter sit-ins: 150 people showed up to Dewey's, demanding service and respect, and handed out flyers to customers. The protests went on for a week, until Dewey's resumed service to all.

1966 On a summer night in San Francisco's Tenderloin District, a group of teenagers marched down the city's downtown thoroughfare with brooms, cleaning trash off the streets in the same way the police had tried to clean them off the streets. These mostly homeless gay and transgender teens were part of Vanguard, America's first gay youth group formed by a local pastor; their action was called the Vanguard Street Sweep. Two months later, the Vanguard youth joined a group of outraged drag queens, gay men, and trans women who fought back when the police tried to kick them out of a popular restaurant called Compton's Cafeteria.

T

IS FOR

TRIANGLE SHIRTWAIST FACTORY

AND THE WOMEN WHO TURNED DISASTER INTO PROGRESS

ON THE EVENING OF November 22, 1909, the Great Hall of the historic Cooper Union building in New York City was hot and crowded. Three thousand people were packed inside, spilling out into the hallways as they listened to speaker after speaker discuss whether to call a general strike to demand better pay and safer conditions for shirtwaist workers. A shirtwaist was a popular kind of woman's blouse at the time, and the workers who made them labored long hours in hot, cramped factories.

Clara Lemlich, age 21, was there in the crowd, and she was fed up. She'd been listening closely, but the speakers were all talk and no *action*. Why didn't they just go ahead and declare a strike? Why keep debating whether workers should continue to accept the brutal conditions of the factories? Clara knew plenty about the suffering of garment workers— she'd been working since age 15, when, like the majority of the other shirtwaist makers, her family had fled anti-Jewish violence in Russia and come to New York's Lower East Side. She knew the backbreaking labor, the meager pay, the cruelty of factory owners. And she knew what could happen when workers speak up: just weeks before, after leading a picket line at a factory, Clara had been violently beaten by two grown men— they broke six of her ribs and left her lying on the sidewalk. They'd been hired by the factory bosses to show what can happen to workers who try to organize.

But Clara's fierce desire for workers' rights couldn't be stopped by hired thugs. Before the next speaker was introduced, she leaped to her feet and screamed in Yiddish (the language spoken by many Eastern European Jews), "I want to say a few words!" The room buzzed—many knew about this young woman who had survived the terrible attack. "Let her speak!" they cried, making way for the five-foot-tall woman with dark eyes and a loud voice. Suddenly she was onstage, in front of thousands.

"I am a working girl, one of those striking against intolerable conditions. I am tired of listening to people speak in generalities. . . . I offer a resolution that a general strike be declared NOW!"

The room erupted in cheers and shouts. Yes, they cried! YES. Clara had done it—a strike was called, right then and there.

THE FOLLOWING MORNING, nearly 20,000 shirtwaist workers all over New York City walked out of their factories, demanding better pay, safer working conditions, and shorter hours. Many of the striking workers were recent immigrants from Russia, Eastern Europe, and Italy—and almost all of them were young women who worked to support their families in New York and abroad. Most of them spoke limited English, and they were taking a huge risk by participating in the strike. The strike received support from other New Yorkers, including members of the Women's Trade Union League (WTUL), a progressive organization of wealthy white women who supported labor reform and women's rights.

The strike, which came to be known as the Uprising of the 20,000, lasted five months, ending in March 1910. While it brought national attention to the struggles of the New York garment workers and showed the power of young immigrant women in the labor movement, it wasn't entirely successful. Although workers received small raises and a promise of fewer hours, no factories agreed to unionize, and not all the factory owners honored the agreements. This was especially true at a factory known as the Triangle Shirtwaist Factory (often shortened to just "Triangle"). Hundreds of workers returned there without contracts— and without the safety measures they'd asked for.

ONE YEAR LATER, on March 25, 1911, it was almost closing time for nearly 500 workers at Triangle, which occupied the top 3 floors of a 10-story skyscraper known as the Asch Building. When the 4:45 p.m. end-of-day bell sounded, the power to the machinery was shut down. On the 8th floor, about 40 men and 100 women finished up their work. Up on the 9th floor, approximately 250 young women, mostly teenagers, began to gather their coats and purses, eager to head home to families and fiancés after a long day of work. Some workers were on the 10th floor, and some had already begun to make their way downstairs.

Suddenly, smoke began to pour from beneath a table on the 8th floor. Was a cigarette tossed onto the ground? Did a burning ember get flicked to the floor? All we know is how quickly it happened: the flames shot up, set fire to paper shirtwaist patterns that hung from the ceiling, then swiftly moved to the flammable piles of scrap fabric that were heaped everywhere. A worker ran to get the hose in the stairwell—but there was no water. It wasn't connected to the standpipe. Within less than a minute, Triangle was ablaze.

The 8th-floor workers rushed down the staircase to one of the exits, and found that the door opened in, instead of out—soon the stairway was too crowded for the girls in front to even open the door. Another group of workers climbed out a window onto the fire escape, but it was cheap, and poorly constructed. The ladder didn't reach the ground, and before anyone could get off, it collapsed.

And on the 9th floor, panicked workers rushed to the nearest exit, only to find that the door was locked. It was a common tactic of factory owners: they locked almost all of the doors to discourage workers from sneaking out early or trying to steal. The fire spread fast, and the workers behind the locked door were trapped. They looked to the windows. They had no choice.

ON THE STREETS OUTSIDE the building, a massive crowd had gathered. They watched, helpless, as the building burned. Objects began to fall from the windows—were they bundles of cloth? No, the horrified onlookers realized: they were bodies. Young women jumping from broken windows to escape the flames.

Sirens wailed in the distance. "Don't jump," cried the people on the street. "Help is on the way!" But it was no use. The desperate girls couldn't hear them above the roar of the blaze. The heat was unbearable. They had to jump. When the firefighters did arrive, their ladders reached only to the 6th floor, and the tarps they used to catch the falling bodies weren't strong enough.

One of the frantic onlookers was a 30-year-old woman named Frances Perkins. She was having tea with friends nearby and came running when she heard the screams and saw the smoke. Once there, she stood and watched in horror. She would never forget what she saw. And though she could do nothing to help while the building burned, she resolved to do everything she could to prevent a disaster like this from happening again.

THE TRIANGLE FIRE, as it would come to be known, burned for less than 30 minutes before it was extinguished. Of the 500 workers who had clocked in that day, 146 perished: 123 women and 23 men. No one who jumped survived, and in the immediate aftermath, nearly 50 bodies lay crumpled on the sidewalk. Most of the dead were teenagers:

the youngest victims were Kate Leone and Rosarea "Sara" Maltese, both 14 years old.

New York City was in a state of shock. The devastation was well-documented: the workers who managed to escape provided harrowing accounts of what it was like inside the inferno, and onlookers gave eyewitness accounts to journalists, whose headlines plastered the front pages of papers. On April 5 nearly 400,000 people turned out on a rainy morning for a massive funeral procession up Fifth Avenue to honor the victims. Many carried banners, including one that read WE MOURN OUR DEAD. Local unions and organizations formed relief committees to support the families of the victims and those injured in the fire. They organized meals and childcare, and, with the help of the Red Cross, a donation fund that sent money to families overseas in Russia and Italy.

But mourning was not enough—it was time for change. Many activists and leaders knew all too well that the deaths could have been prevented if the demands of the striking unions had been listened to—and enforced. People like Frances Perkins, who had been actively working to stop child labor before the fire, were wracked with guilt, feeling that they could and should have done more to prevent such a tragedy.

A WEEK AFTER THE FIRE, hundreds attended a mass meeting at the Metropolitan Opera House to discuss fire safety and workplace reform. The room was filled with social reformers, grieving workers, millionaire socialites, and rabble-rousing union leaders. Frances Perkins was there, and so was a redheaded woman named Rose Schneiderman, a prominent member of the WTUL who had dropped out of school to work in a factory after sixth grade. Some people proposed asking the city to create a Bureau of Fire Prevention, but others in the crowd thought that wasn't enough. They didn't trust the city officials to really do anything. They wanted more—they wanted *action*. And like Clara Lemlich, so did Rose, who stepped forward and delivered a spontaneous speech:

"This is not the first time girls have been burned alive in the city. Every year thousands of us are maimed. . . . Too much blood has been spilled. I know from my experience it is up to the working people to save themselves!"

Like Clara's speech that had kicked off the Uprising, Rose's impassioned account sparked a new energy in the meeting, and the prominent leaders onstage pledged to immediately form a citizen's commission to demand reform. A number of powerful men were appointed to the committee, but it was Frances who led the charge.

Frances's first move was to go straight to Al Smith, one of the most powerful men in New York City, who would later become governor. She wanted action, and he listened. The New York Factory Investigating Commission (FIC) was formed, and Frances was named the lead investigator. Her staff included prominent labor leaders like Mary Dreier of the WTUL, as well as Clara and Rose. Over the next four years, the commission fanned out across the entire state of New York, investigating 3,385 workplaces, interviewing nearly 500 workers and owners, and producing more than 7,000 pages of first-person testimony, including statements from five-year-old children found

working alongside their parents in a canning factory. The commission even brought wealthy politicians into dark, cramped factories to witness the conditions firsthand.

THE FIC'S EFFORTS RESULTED in 38 new labor laws. All high-rise buildings had to have automatic sprinklers. Fire drills became mandatory. Exit doors had to open *out*, not *in*. New policies were put in place to make sure these laws were actually enforced. New York emerged from an unthinkable tragedy with the most comprehensive set of labor laws in the country.

Clara and Rose both devoted the rest of their lives to the rights of workers and particularly of women. Rose became head of the New York State Department of Labor, and when her good friend Eleanor Roosevelt's husband became president, Rose helped influence major national policy—including the creation of Social Security. Clara, blacklisted from factory work due to her activism, joined the

Communist Party, organized tenants, led rent strikes, and unionized housewives. In 1935 she founded the United Council of Working-Class Housewives, which supported the wives of men who were on strike. She helped the women raise funds, gather food, and set up community kitchens and cooperative child care.

In 1933 President Roosevelt appointed Frances Perkins as the first Secretary of Labor. She was the first woman to hold a cabinet position, and she is considered one of the main architects of FDR's New Deal. She was a driving force behind policies that transformed American life, including the 40-hour work week, a minimum wage, unemployment compensation, and the abolition of child labor.

The Triangle Fire opened the nation's eyes to the gruesome reality of sweatshop labor and the exploitation of workers, especially young immigrants and women. It strengthened the labor movement and set in motion a new era of workplace reform and safety. Did it result in justice for all? Unfortunately, no: the two owners of the Triangle Factory were found innocent by an all-male jury. Did it end the problems facing workers in America? Absolutely not. Those struggles continue today. Workers, especially immigrant and undocumented workers, are still exploited, and unions still come under threat and criticism for demanding safety and fairness for their members. But the movement for justice and fairness still thrives, as workers and unions stand together, aware of their histories and confident in their futures.

T IS ALSO FOR . . .

TAKE BACK THE NIGHT: An annual event that takes place in communities all over the world to bring attention to and end all forms of sexual violence.

TEATRO CAMPESINO: A California-based Chicano theater company founded in 1965. The cultural arm of the United Farm Workers, the company performed political theater at rallies and marches, and along picket lines.

THIRD WORLD LIBERATION FRONT: A coalition of various ethnic student groups on California college campuses whose successful 1968 strike led to the hiring of more faculty of color, the admission of more students of color, and the creation of ethnic studies classes and departments.

TITLE IX: Part of the Educational Amendments Act of 1972 that affirms the equal treatment of the sexes in higher education. Pioneered and sponsored by Congresswoman Patsy Mink, it helped level the playing field for women's collegiate sports.

U

IS FOR

UNITED FARM WORKERS

Y LA LUCHA POR LOS TRABAJADORES EN LOS CAMPOS

"¡Sí, se puede!" ("Yes, we can!")

—DOLORES HUERTA, COFOUNDER OF UNITED FARM WORKERS

THE STATE OF CALIFORNIA is one of America's—and the world's—leading producers of fruits and vegetables. It's where nearly all of the country's artichokes, lettuce, broccoli, avocados, olives, tomatoes, apricots, strawberries, and grapes come from. Historically, the growers—the people who owned the fields, ranches, and orchards where the produce was grown—were among the richest and most powerful people in the state. But the workers who planted, tended, and harvested the produce were some of the most underpaid, disrespected, and mistreated. This was the case for nearly 100 years, until a historic workers' strike in the vineyards of California's Central Valley set in motion the most significant campaign in modern labor history: the farmworker movement.

California's Central Valley region has summer temperatures that reach 110 degrees or more, and workers usually toiled from sunrise to sunset, sometimes sharing one jug of water and a single cup. There were no restrooms and no breaks. Workers had no healthcare and no protections if they were injured on the job. Because many of the crops, like lettuce and strawberries, grew low to the ground, workers developed physical problems from stooping over all day. Toxic pesticides sickened many workers and their children and unborn babies. The children of migrant workers rarely finished school, and the average life expectancy of a farmworker at this time was 49 years: 20 years shorter than the average working American's life expectancy. By the 1960s, many felt the situation was unbearable, and some skilled and committed leaders were ready to make change happen.

THROUGHOUT THE COUNTRY, the civil rights movement was giving new energy to oppressed communities seeking change, and there was growing interest in new strategies for nonviolent organizing. The Agricultural Workers Organizing Committee (AWOC), a mostly Filipino workers' rights group, was founded in 1959 by two activists named Larry Itliong and Dolores Huerta. Dolores, a mother of 11 who was one of the only female lobbyists in Sacramento, had also cofounded the National Farm Workers Association

(NFWA)—a similar organization comprised of mostly Mexican American farmworkers—with a charismatic leader and organizer named Cesar Chavez. These three leaders—Dolores, Larry, and Cesar—joined forces to build a historic movement, organizing their fellow farmworkers to join the struggle for better pay and safe working conditions.

On September 8, 1965, Larry and other AWOC members officially called for a strike against grape growers in the small farming town of Delano, California. The workers wanted to be paid minimum wage and to be able to form a union to negotiate fair contracts. Larry led more than a thousand Filipino workers as they walked off the grape farms to picket in protest.

This was a bold step for the workers, but Larry anticipated that the Filipino workers would likely just be replaced by Mexican workers. This was a classic technique: growers would pit the two ethnic communities against each other to break strikes. If the Filipino workers complained about low wages, the owners of the farms would just hire Mexican workers and shut out the Filipinos, and vice versa. Larry knew his strike wouldn't succeed unless the two communities could come together and organize as one.

As the Filipino workers walked off the job, a young Mexican laborer named Esther Uranday watched them. At age 28, Esther had been working in the fields for more than 20 years, picking cotton, plums, apricots, and potatoes across California with her family. Esther had been one of the very first members of the NFWA—and she knew this strike was a big deal. She rushed to tell Cesar and Dolores that the Filipinos were striking—and to urge them to join the strike.

Cesar didn't think the Mexican workers were ready for a strike. The NFWA had about $100 in its bank account, not enough to buy supplies and support the strikers. But they put it to a vote. On September 16, 1965, Mexican Independence Day, hundreds of Latino farmworkers packed into a church in Delano to vote on whether or not to join Filipino workers on the picket line. It was a unanimous *yes* vote, and the chapel was filled with chants of "*Huelga! Huelga!*"—the Spanish word for "strike."

THE AWOC AND THE NFWA decided to join together, and an unexpected and powerful coalition was born: the United Farm Workers (UFW). Within a week, thousands of workers had joined the picket line. The organizers worked hard to make the strike as effective as possible, waking up hours before dawn to drive from farm to farm and urge workers to join the strike.

It wasn't an easy task. Many of the workers didn't think the strike would be worth it or that it would actually be possible to improve their working conditions, believing the farm owners simply had too much power. The organizers got into intense confrontations with the farm owners, who tried to keep them from talking to the workers. And many of the protesting workers were arrested. On one particular day 44 strikers, including Esther and 13 other women, were arrested for standing outside of a vineyard yelling, "*Huelga! Huelga!*"

Before long word had spread, and the strike began to gain support from outside the Central Valley. Dolores was the lead negotiator in meetings with hostile growers and skeptical politicians, known for being tough and persuasive. Cesar used his charisma

launched a boycott: a massive, nonviolent effort to convince as many people as possible to stop buying California-grown grapes until the growers agreed to the workers' demands.

To prepare for the boycott, organizers looked to examples of successful boycotts from history, including Mahatma Gandhi's salt boycott in India in the 1930s and the Montgomery Bus Boycott of 1956. They knew that boycotts could be effective, but only if they were strategic and well organized. For the grape boycott to have an impact it would have to be nationwide—but asking a family in Massachusetts to boycott grapes so poor California workers could be paid more felt impossible. They would need *a lot* of help in order to pull it off.

UFW members began to travel across the country to share their stories and appeal directly to their fellow Americans— especially the women. They knew that if consumers could connect real faces and voices to the cause, they'd be more likely to think twice when reaching for grapes at the grocery store. They recruited thousands of additional volunteers for the effort, from high school and college students to antiwar activists and suburban housewives. All the new recruits went through rigorous training: they learned how to make outreach phone calls, ask for donations, be polite yet persuasive, and follow up with contacts.

Around 40 cities were targeted for the initial boycott in the hope that the message would spread from there into other cities and towns. At hundreds—even thousands—of supermarkets, a UFW volunteer would stand outside, talking about their efforts and asking people to pledge their support of the

and speaking skills to win public support, inspiring more workers to join *la causa* (the cause). Six months after the strike began, Cesar led a 340-mile march from Delano to Sacramento, California's state capital, to speak to state lawmakers about the strike, to get the public's attention, and to raise funds to support the striking workers and their families. The *peregrinación*, or "pilgrimage," began with about 70 people; by the time the march reached Sacramento on Easter Sunday, there were thousands of marchers, and more than 10,000 supporters waited there to greet them. The UFW was proving that it was more than a union—it was a civil rights movement.

IT WAS TIME TO take the fight for farmworkers' rights to the next level: in 1967, with the grape growers strike still in effect, the UFW boycott. Other volunteers set up tables on busy streets or college campuses, or walked door to door in residential neighborhoods, handing out information and pledge cards asking for support. They passed out flyers that read "Please remember the Farmworker, who harvests your food. Please don't buy grapes!" In Spanish, *Uvas no!* means "No grapes!"—and that's the phrase that began to appear on bumper stickers, buttons, and protest signs.

DOLORES WAS IN CHARGE of coordinating the boycott in New York, where she formed an important alliance with feminist leader Gloria Steinem. In private homes in cities like Boston and Philadelphia, the women of the UFW met with local mothers and housewives to tell their stories. By explaining their struggle directly to these women—who did most of the grocery shopping and food preparation for their families—they were able to build even more support. Many suburban women came to feel personally connected to the California workers, and spread the message to their friends and neighbors. This house-by-house approach was an important part of Dolores's and Cesar's organizing strategy. It was time-consuming, but it was worth it. The boycott began to catch on, as more and more Americans stopped buying grapes.

Many of the farmworkers-turned-organizers had never before left their small towns, let alone the state of California; for many of them, the boycott was a life-changing experience. A woman named Jessica Govea, who had begun working in the fields at age 4, joined the UFW at age 19. Two years later, Jessica was sent from California to Toronto to organize the grape boycott in Canada, one of the top five markets for California grapes. She had never traveled outside of her small

hometown, but she made a huge impression on the Canadians, giving public speeches about the treatment of Mexican workers and convincing three major grocery chains to stop selling grapes.

The mayor of Toronto proclaimed "Grape Day" in official support of the boycott, and Jessica went on to coordinate the boycott in Montreal and the entire province of Quebec—where nearly 75 percent of the population spoke French. Jessica grew up speaking Spanish and hadn't even become proficient in English until high school. But she recruited bilingual local volunteers and got Quebec on board with the boycott too. Eventually Jessica became the UFW's national director of organizing and an executive board member.

The grape boycott lasted for five long years. In 1968, when growers began using violence against striking workers, Cesar embarked on a hunger strike, refusing to eat for 25 days to bring attention to the UFW's commitment to nonviolence. He broke the fast when he was joined by then-senator Robert F. Kennedy, who spoke of Cesar's courage and the need to respect the farmworkers. As Cesar ate a piece of bread, someone read these words for him: "It is how we use our lives that determines what kind of men we are. . . . I am convinced that the truest act of courage, the strongest act of manliness, is to sacrifice ourselves for others in a totally nonviolent struggle for justice."

By the end of the 1960s, the boycott was working: untouched grapes were rotting in grocery store produce sections, and growers were losing money fast. The success of the Canadian boycott put even more pressure on the growers. And finally, in July 1970, the California grape growers recognized the UFW as a legitimate union and signed union contracts granting workers better pay, benefits, and protections. Soon stickers with the UFW logo—a black eagle with wings shaped like an upside-down Aztec pyramid—began appearing on packages of supermarket grapes picked by union members. These stickers told consumers across North America that the grapes had been picked by union members, and they were okay to purchase.

The work of the UFW to organize for workers' rights would continue for the next several decades, with many successes and challenges. But the grape boycott—America's first successful consumer boycott—left an indelible mark on labor and civil rights history.

U IS ALSO FOR . . .

"UNBOUGHT AND UNBOSSED": The slogan for the 1972 campaign of Representative Shirley Chisholm, the first black woman to run for president.

UNDERGROUND RAILROAD: A network of safe houses and routes established in the US in the early to mid-1800s, used by enslaved people to escape into free states and Canada.

UNION OF CONCERNED SCIENTISTS: A nonprofit science advocacy organization, founded in 1969, that seeks to use the power of science to address global issues like climate change, nuclear weapons, corporate corruption, and poverty.

UNITED STATES V. WONG KIM ARK: An 1898 Supreme Court ruling that granted birthright citizenship for all babies born in the US, no matter what country their parents are from.

UNIVERSAL DECLARATION OF HUMAN RIGHTS: The world's first international bill of rights, published in 1948 and adopted by the United Nations General Assembly; the committee that drafted it was overseen by Eleanor Roosevelt.

V

IS FOR
VOTING RIGHTS

AND THE LONG JOURNEY TOWARD SUFFRAGE FOR ALL

VOTING IS ONE OF the key pillars of a democratic society. Despite that, the question of who gets to vote in America has long been a complicated one. The Constitution leaves it up to the states to decide, and the laws have changed over the years. More than half of the original 13 states allowed free black men to vote. In Pennsylvania, black men could vote until 1838, when the state amended its constitution to allow only "white freemen" to vote. And women and black men could vote in the state of New Jersey until 1807, when the state legislature changed the law. But by 1820 or so, most states had narrowed their restrictions on who gets to vote, ensuring that those who got to participate in democracy were white landowning men who paid

taxes. (During the first presidential election in 1789, that was only about 6 percent of the population.)

In the two centuries since then, women, poor white people, African Americans, Native Americans, Latinos, Asian Americans, and many immigrants have fought for the full enfranchisement (ability to vote) of all people. They've marched, chanted, testified, and organized. They've held rallies, conventions, sit-ins, and workshops. They've been beaten and harassed, arrested and imprisoned, and some have lost their lives. Many never gave up—even in the face of violence.

ON JANUARY 10, 1917, a group of white women stood silently in front of the White House in Washington, DC. It was freezing cold: they wore heavy coats, gloves, and scarves. They also wore sashes in gold, purple, and white: the colors of the women's suffrage movement. The day before, 300 suffrage activists had met with President Woodrow Wilson, hoping to convince him to finally grant American women the right to vote.

But President Wilson brushed off their impassioned pleas, arguing that he was focused on World War I and whether or not the US should fight for freedom overseas. *Why should we fight for another country's democracy*, the women asked, *when more than half of America can't even vote?* The activists, who were members of the National Women's Party, vowed to show up at the White House every day until President Wilson changed his mind.

And they did, beginning on that freezing January day. They returned the next day, and the next, becoming the first people ever to picket the White House in protest. They called themselves the Silent Sentinels, and they showed up six days a week for nearly two years. More than 2,000 women traveled to Washington, DC, from 30 states to take their turns on the picket line and help with the ongoing demonstration.

They stood there despite rain, snow, and freezing temperatures, as well as harassment from disrespectful onlookers, and eventually the police, who began to arrest the women for blocking the sidewalk. After the US entered World War I in April 1917, public sentiment shifted, and many saw the protests as unpatriotic. Some of the original picketers agreed, and stopped showing up. But other women—especially working-class women and labor activists—remained, refusing to back down.

THEN CAME THE NIGHT of Terror. In November 1917, a group of 33 Sentinels were arrested and sent to Occoquan Workhouse, a prison in Virginia. By this time, many of the women had been sent there a number of times already. The superintendent of the prison knew who they were, and he wanted to teach them a lesson. He authorized his prison guards to attack them.

Dora Lewis was knocked unconscious when guards smashed her head against an iron bed. Dorothy Day, who went on to become a prominent Catholic activist, was slammed onto a metal bench, her arms twisted behind her. Lucy Burns was forced to stand all night, her wrists shackled to the wall. Julia Emory raised her hands, too, assuming the same painful position in solidarity. Alice Cosu had a heart attack and collapsed. The guards refused to give her medical treatment and wouldn't let her friends help her. They thought she was dead.

The women in Occuquan were denied access to attorneys, but word of the attacks got out to the newspapers, and at least one member of President Wilson's cabinet resigned over the treatment of the women. A judge finally ordered the women to be released from the prison—and they resumed their protests immediately. Within a few months, in January 1918, President Wilson called on Congress to act on the federal suffrage amendment.

The amendment failed to pass several times, despite President Wilson's appeals. But on August 18, 1920, Tennessee narrowly approved it when 24-year-old Harry Burn, the youngest member of the state legislature, changed his vote from "nay" to "aye" at the very last minute, giving the amendment the one vote it needed to pass.

Harry had received a letter from his mother asking him to "be a good boy" and "vote for suffrage!" He listened to his mother—and to the thousands of women who had devoted their lives to the cause. The Nineteenth Amendment was finally added to the United States Constitution.

THE PASSAGE OF THE Nineteenth Amendment was the culmination of a historic struggle—but the fight for voting rights in America was not over. To understand, we have to go back in time. The decade following the Civil War is known as the Reconstruction Era: the period between 1865 and 1877 when America attempted to reconstruct itself in the wake of a devastating war. In 1865 Congress ratified the Thirteenth Amendment, officially abolishing slavery and ushering in a wave of new laws, including the Reconstruction Act of 1867. To ensure that the new laws were followed, the federal government sent military troops into Southern states.

During Reconstruction, many black Americans thrived: families were reunited;

homes were purchased; businesses, churches, and prosperous communities were established; and art forms like the Blues and Jazz flourished. Perhaps most notably, black men gained immense political power. After the passage of the Fifteenth Amendment in 1870, more than half a million black men became voters.

Between 1870 and the late 1880s, 17 black men were elected to the U.S. Congress, and more than 600 were elected to state legislatures. Hundreds held local offices all across the South, serving as court clerks, sheriffs, city council members, coroners, auditors, and registrars. Black men worked with white Republican politicians to write new state constitutions, undoing decades of racist policies, establishing public school systems, and doing away with the post–Civil War "black codes" that attempted to restrict the freedom of newly freed and freeborn black citizens.

But with these enormous advances came enormous backlash. The Union won the war, but that didn't mean white Southerners changed their minds about slavery. Many Southerners—and the Southern Democrats in the House and Senate—fought hard to regain economic, political, and cultural supremacy. They used violence and lynching—and political bargaining. The too-close-to-call presidential election of 1876 was resolved with the Compromise of 1877: Republican Rutherford B. Hayes became president, but his party agreed to withdraw all federal troops from Southern states, effectively ending Reconstruction.

AS THE 19TH CENTURY came to a close, white Southern Democrats regained control, and the Southern states saw the creation of numerous regulations known as Jim Crow laws (named after a popular racist song sung by white comedians in blackface) intended to reinstate white supremacy and limit the freedoms that black citizens gained during Reconstruction. One of the most effective strategies to achieve these dubious goals was to prevent black men from registering to vote. If you weren't registered to vote, you couldn't serve on a jury—and you couldn't run for office. You had no political power whatsoever.

State and local officials found all kinds of ways to pass unfair, restrictive voter laws without legally violating the Constitution, including poll taxes, literacy tests, and residency requirements. A "grandfather clause" said that if your father or grandfather had voted in the last election before the abolition of slavery, then you didn't have to pay the poll tax or take the literacy test. But a newly free black person's father wouldn't have had the right to vote, and most newly freed black people had never been allowed to learn to read.

By 1910 all of the former Confederate states had new laws disenfranchising non-white and poor white voters. Only 730 black men were registered to vote in the state of Louisiana, even though they made up the majority of the state's population. The number of black men in Congress and statewide offices plummeted. The 1896 Supreme Court case *Plessy v. Ferguson* had upheld segregation as constitutional, giving a new legitimacy to Jim Crow laws.

In the years before and after World War I, many states passed laws barring non-citizens from voting, which directly impacted Native American men and women, who weren't granted full citizenship until 1924, as well as Mexican laborers in the West and Southwest, and immigrants of Asian descent, who weren't able to become naturalized citizens until 1952. Literacy tests persisted in many states, preventing non-native English speakers from registering as well.

DURING THE 1950s AND 1960s, tens of thousands of participants in the civil rights movement fought for justice, equality, and the right to safely and freely cast a ballot. It was the enduring efforts of civil rights activists like Ella Baker, Diane Nash, Amelia Boynton, and a woman named Fannie Lou Hamer that resulted in the historic and long-overdue expansion of voting rights.

On August 22, 1964, Fannie Lou—who, like many black women who'd fought hard for their dignity,

preferred to be addressed as Mrs. Hamer— was in New Jersey at the Democratic National Convention with the Mississippi Freedom Democratic Party (MFDP), an integrated coalition of delegates that she had helped to create. Mrs. Hamer and the 67 other delegates had spent the summer working with civil rights activists to build this new political party and to register black voters across the state. Their efforts, known as the Freedom Summer, were a key campaign in the ongoing struggle for civil rights.

Political conventions are held so party members can decide which candidate to support in a presidential election, and to determine the "platform," or priorities, of the political party. Each state sends a delegation, and

Mrs. Hamer and the MFDP had come to challenge the all-white Democratic delegation from Mississippi, most of whom supported segregation. The MFDP believed *they* should be "seated" (allowed to participate) at this crucial convention instead of the racist politicians. In order to be seated, representatives from the MFDP would have to testify in front of a committee and try to convince them of this. They knew it wouldn't be an easy task.

The room was packed with people, and the committee hearing was broadcast live on television. Rita Schwerner, the widow of slain civil rights activist Michael Schwerner, testified. Then Dr. Martin Luther King Jr. spoke, and then came Mrs. Hamer, a sharecropper from rural Mississippi with a sixth-grade education who was there to tell the crowd—and everyone watching on television—exactly what happens when a black woman tries to register to vote in Mississippi.

Mrs. Hamer had begun her journey to become one of America's leading human rights activists only two years earlier. In 1962 she showed up to a meeting in her small town of Ruleville, Mississippi, to learn about voter registration. The meeting had been organized by the Student Nonviolent Coordinating Committee (SNCC), a nationwide network of civil rights activists committed to increasing black voter registration. They'd come to Ruleville hoping to connect with folks like Mrs. Hamer, who lived with her husband on a plantation, in a shack with no electricity or indoor plumbing.

Mrs. Hamer had been hearing about the civil rights movement and wanted to know more. As she listened to the SNCC volunteer speak about the importance of voting, she learned something that changed her life: all black people had the right to vote. It was written in the Constitution, right there in the Fifteenth and Nineteenth amendments. She'd had no idea. At the end of the meeting, Mrs. Hamer raised her hand to volunteer. Soon she was leading workshops, registering voters, and traveling—and she was nearly beaten to death in a prison cell because of it.

MRS. HAMER'S VOICE WAS loud and powerful. For 13 full minutes at the committee hearing, she described exactly what she had been through, beginning with her first attempt to register to vote when she and 17 others took a 26-mile bus ride to the courthouse. City officials allowed only Mrs. Hamer and one other person inside to take the literacy test. They failed the test, which included obscure questions about the state constitution that most people wouldn't know. On the way home, police pulled over the bus and fined the driver.

She explained what happened when she got home: her boss had heard about her attempt to register. "We're not ready for that here in Mississippi," he said, and she replied, "I didn't try to register for you; I tried to register for myself." She was fired, and had to leave that night. The following week, someone shot 16 bullets into the home where she was staying.

Then came the most intense part of her testimony. One day, she was traveling home from a voting rights workshop in South Carolina with a group of activists. They were confronted by police, taken to county jail, and brutally beaten. As Mrs. Hamer told this part of the story, her voice became louder. She explained in detail how the prison guards forced two other black inmates to beat her and another young woman. How she didn't think she'd survive. How she lost partial sight in her left eye and sustained permanent kidney damage. How a few days later she learned of the death of her close friend, the activist Medgar Evers, who was murdered by a white supremacist.

By this point, Mrs. Hamer's eyes had teared up. There was a slight tremor in her booming voice as she looked at her audience and said, "All of this is on account of we want to register, to become first-class citizens. And if the Freedom Democratic Party is not seated now, I question America. Is this America? The land of the free and the home of the brave, where . . . our lives are threatened daily, because we want to live as decent human beings?"

When she finished, the stunned audience went from complete silence to thunderous applause. In telling her story, Mrs. Hamer had told the story of so many black Americans who, even in the 1960s, were still living under Jim Crow laws.

Later that day, Mrs. Hamer and the delegates learned something infuriating: President Johnson had been so afraid of what Mrs. Hamer was going to say that he called an emergency press conference so the television networks would cut away from her speech to cover him instead. But his plan ended up backfiring: while Americans didn't see her entire speech live, the fact that her broadcast was cut short became a big story, and her testimony was played in full on the evening news that night by the three major television networks. Mrs. Hamer's story was in the homes of families across the country.

Mrs. Hamer's testimony brought the truth about voter suppression and anti-black violence into the living rooms—and consciousness—of America. Once her words were broadcast widely, national politicians could no longer deny that the constitutional rights of black Americans in Mississippi, Alabama, and other Southern states were being violated.

THE MISSISSIPPI FREEDOM PARTY did not get what they wanted at that convention. They were offered a compromise of two seats (while the "official" delegation of segregationist politicians all got seats). "We didn't come all this way for no two seats when all of us is tired," Mrs. Hamer argued, and the delegation rejected it. They were furious, but their challenge to the political establishment, combined with Mrs. Hamer's powerful speech, marked a turning point in the civil rights movement. The next year would bring some of the most intense conflicts of all, especially in Alabama. But it would also bring one of the most significant victories: seven months after Mrs. Hamer's testimony, President Johnson introduced the Voting Rights Act of 1965.

This landmark piece of federal legislation prohibited racial discrimination in voting, and gave the federal government authority to dismantle Jim Crow laws like poll taxes and literacy tests. It was signed into law on August 6, 1965: 100 years after the end of the Civil War, and 45 years after the ratification of the Nineteenth Amendment. The impact was immediate: in 1965, 6.7 percent of eligible black voters in Mississippi were registered to vote. By 1967, that number was almost 60 percent, and five decades later, in 2012, it was 90.2 percent.

In 1975, thanks to the efforts of the Mexican American Legal Defense and Education Fund (MALDEF) and other activists, President Gerald Ford signed an extension of the Voting Rights Act that ended discrimination against "language minorities" and required voting materials to be translated into other languages. This finally enabled millions of non-English speaking US residents to participate in democracy, and led to major political empowerment in Latino communities across the nation. That same year, activist Willie Velasquez founded the Southwest Voter Education Project, which aimed to register as many Latino voters as possible.

LITERACY TESTS AND POLL taxes are now illegal, but states and counties have continued to pass laws and restrictions that make it harder for people (especially nonwhite people, poor people, and immigrants) to vote. Tactics include gerrymandering (manipulating the boundaries of voting districts to include or exclude specific communities and to favor one particular political party); voter ID laws (requiring official government-issued identification to vote; approximately 1 in 10 Americans don't have this kind of ID); closing or limiting polling places in rural areas and communities of color; and eliminating or reducing early voting and absentee ballots, which disproportionately impacts communities of color, rural residents, and disabled and elderly voters.

In 2013 the Supreme Court struck down a key part of the Voting Rights Act. The conservative justices who made that decision argued, in part, that the Voting Rights Act had worked, so it wasn't needed anymore. Justice Ruth Bader Ginsburg strongly disagreed, writing that throwing out a law that has worked and is continuing to work is like "throwing away your umbrella in a rainstorm because you are not getting wet."

New generations of activists agree, and they are continuing to preserve the legacy of the suffragists, the Silent Sentinels, the civil rights visionaries, and all of the communities who have fought—and still fight—to ensure that *all* eligible voters get to be part of their democracy.

V IS ALSO FOR . . .

VICTORY GARDENS: Vegetable, herb, and fruit gardens planted at homes and on public lands during World War I and World War II to help feed local communities and to boost morale during wartime.

VIETNAM WAR PROTESTS: The near-decade of marches, demonstrations, teach-ins, and public protests to oppose US involvement in the Vietnam War beginning on college campuses in the early 1960s and lasting until the early 1970s, when President Richard Nixon formally withdrew US troops. In addition to opposing the war itself, many protesters were also resisting the draft, the American system of forced military enlistment that disproportionately impacted poor and nonwhite young men.

VOGUEING: A form of stylized dance movements that originated in New York City in the 1970s and '80s among the predominantly black and Latino gay communities in Harlem.

IS FOR
WITCHES

AND THE POWER AND PERSECUTION OF WOMEN

"A witch lives and laughs in every woman.
She is the free part of each of us."
—FROM THE 1969 W.I.T.C.H. MANIFESTO

WITCHES HAVE ALWAYS EXISTED. They still do. They are present on every continent, and their work—and magic—takes many different forms. Witches might dance, sing, pray, chant, conjure, commune, or heal. They might use rituals, spells, or chants; herbs, roots, flowers, or potions. They practice in solitude, with covens, with their ancestors, and in online communities. In some cultures, witches are revered and respected. More often, though, they are feared—and persecuted.

Witches appear in Greek mythology, from the powerful Circe in Homer's epic *The Odyssey*, to ancient myths about Hecate, the goddess of witchcraft, light, and magic. They appear in the Old Testament, in which the Witch of Endor is summoned by Saul, and in Shakespeare, whose trio of witches chant "double, double toil and trouble" over their magical cauldron in *Macbeth*. And *Grimm's Fairy Tales* gives us the child-eating witch of "Hansel and Gretel," among others.

Witches are everywhere in American popular culture: tempting and scary in Disney's version of the Grimm's *Snow White*, and wicked *and* good in *The Wizard of Oz.* Halloween brings pointed hats and broomsticks to neighborhoods all over America. During the 2016 election, photoshopped images of Democratic candidate Hillary Clinton as an ugly witch were shared across social media platforms by people who didn't like her.

No matter what your interpretation is— sweet or spooky, cruel or kind—the vision of a witch is almost always a woman. Men can be witches too (whether called warlocks, wizards, or also witches) but, in the words of historian Carol Karlsen, "the story of witchcraft is primarily a story of women."

FOR MANY AMERICANS, the Salem Witch Trials are the starting point for real witch history. The story of what happened in the small colonial village of Salem, Massachusetts, between 1692 and 1693 remains fascinating more than 300 years after it happened. How did a tight-knit, deeply religious community end up accusing more than 200 of its own people of witchcraft and dealing with the devil, executing 20 of them within the span of one bleak year?

The events in Salem began with three young girls who reported experiencing strange fits of screaming, making weird sounds, and contorting their bodies into unusual positions. The local doctor blamed these fits on the devil, and under pressure from village leaders, the girls accused three local women of witchcraft.

The people of Salem were Puritans who had separated from the Church of England and come to New England in the 17th century. Their strict religious lifestyle laid the foundation for their colonial religious and social life. Puritans believed that witches had made a pact with the devil, so not only were witches a threat to man, but they were also a threat to God. The Puritans closely followed the Bible, in which they read "Thou shalt not suffer a witch to live" (Exodus 22:18) and "A man also or woman that hath a familiar spirit, or that is a wizard, shall surely be put to death" (Leviticus 20:27). They took these passages literally.

Despite a complete lack of evidence, all three accused women were executed. But the accusations didn't end with them. Paranoia spread rapidly, as villagers in Salem and neighboring towns began pointing fingers at others who seemed suspicious or out of the ordinary, or whose lifestyles threatened the strict social order. Neighbors accused neighbors; friends accused friends. The frenzy of accusations, counter-accusations, confessions, denials, trials, and executions consumed—and nearly destroyed—several New England communities.

Scholars have tried for centuries to explain how and why this happened. Some suggested it was God punishing the town, others blamed a sudden mental illness, and one theory even suggested that a fungus that grows on rye bread caused psychedelic hallucinations. There may not be a single explanation; most likely a number of factors came together to create what playwright Arthur Miller called a "crucible" (an intense situation in which something new is formed) in his play of the same name, a dramatized version of the Salem trials.

BUT AMERICAN WITCH TRIALS didn't just happen in Salem. Persecutions and accusations of witchcraft happened all over New England during the 17th and 18th centuries. The first known execution of an accused witch in New England took place in Connecticut in 1647, with the hanging of 40-year-old Alyse Young.

Between 1620 and 1725, 344 residents of New England were accused of witchcraft. Nearly 80 percent of them were female— and about half of the accused men were the husbands, sons, or close friends of the accused women. While children as young as 4 were accused, most of the accused women were over age 40. They were more likely to be single, widowed, or divorced; many were poor, but a number of the accused owned property (which was not common for women at the time). Some were healers or midwives; others were just flat-out disliked. In other words, nearly all of the women accused of witchcraft were living lives that were *different* from the rigid structure of the Puritan community. And that may have been the real reason they were punished.

In the late 19th century, feminist writer Matilda Joslyn Gage offered a radical new perspective on the New England witch hunts in her book *Woman, Church and State,* a detailed analysis of the history of Christian patriarchy (the social system in which men hold the power). Her chapter on witchcraft examines the ways in which women have been accused, tortured, and killed under the guise of punishing "witchcraft" and "wickedness" for centuries. Matilda, a leading activist for suffrage, argued that a witch was not necessarily evil but "a woman of superior knowledge." And that was seen as a threat.

The New England witch hunts weren't, she argued, about exorcising the devil. They were about controlling women, and they were part of a deep misogyny and fear of women that goes back many, many centuries. Matilda's ideas about witches didn't just influence feminist scholars—her devoted son-in-law, L. Frank Baum, was so inspired by her theories that he created four witches—two good and two wicked—in his book *The Wizard of Oz*.

OF COURSE, THE NEW ENGLAND witch hunts did not actually eliminate witchcraft and magic in America. Traditions and practices of healing, magic, and witchcraft have endured for centuries, often being passed down through the generations and taught in homes, in nature, and sometimes in quiet, secret ways. They've also journeyed with people who've left homelands and moved around the globe.

The indigenous people who originally inhabited America had complex systems of magic, healing, and spirituality. People who arrived in America—whether by force or by choice—often brought their own practices, which then developed over time in their new country. This includes those who were kidnapped and forcibly brought to America in the transatlantic slave trade. Many enslaved people from West Africa, Brazil, Haiti, and other Afro-Caribbean nations retained their traditions, going to great lengths to hide their practices from slaveholders who feared their magic.

Over time, these traditions mixed with the Western religions that many enslaved people were forced to adopt, as well as the spiritual practices of other enslaved people and the folk magic of immigrants from other

countries. This has resulted in *syncretic*, or blended, practices, including Cuban Santería, Brazilian Candomblé, Mexican *brujería*, Haitian Vodou, New Orleans Hoodoo (also known as rootwork or Conjure), and more. European immigrant traditions include Pennsylvania Dutch pow-wow, Appalachian "granny magic," and Ozark folk magic.

Practitioners of these forms were not necessarily called witches, of course; they might have been called root doctors, *curanderos*, granny women, yarb doctors, lay healers, or cunning folk. In many cases, these practices were passed down from ancestors and emerged out of necessity. To heal the injured, tend to the sick and dying, and deliver and care for babies, people used all the tools and tricks they had.

IN THE MID-20TH CENTURY, new forms of modern witchcraft began to develop in America. Wicca is a contemporary Pagan movement that started in England in the 1950s and was introduced to the US in the mid-1960s. Though it was a newly invented form of witchcraft and religion, it was rooted in ancient European traditions and occult practices.

In 1968 Wicca combined with the countercultural and feminist movements when a group of activists formed a group called W.I.T.C.H. (Women's International Terrorist Conspiracy from Hell). W.I.T.C.H. members embraced the popular image of broom-riding, black-clad witches in pointy hats and engaged in political public performance and guerrilla theater.

On Halloween 1968, W.I.T.C.H. members dressed in black, put on scary makeup, and marched down Wall Street in New York to hex the Stock Exchange in protest of capitalist greed. (The Dow Jones average dropped several points the next day!) W.I.T.C.H.

covens started up in cities like Boston, San Francisco, and Chicago, where witch-outfitted members continued the public pranks. They released white mice inside a bridal fair to protest the idea that all women need to get married; they put a spell on the Chicago Federal Building during the trial of protesters arrested during the Democratic National Convention; and they traveled to Washington, DC, in 1969 to hex the inauguration of the newly elected president, Richard Nixon. W.I.T.C.H. lasted for only a few years, but it had an impact on the idea that feminist activism and witchcraft could—and should—be connected.

IN 2016 WITCHES—and W.I.T.C.H.—began to rise up and resist in newly activated ways. In the wake of the 2016 election and the racist, xenophobic policies of the new political administration, groups of witches in several cities started new activist covens based on the original W.I.T.C.H. organization. Committed to intersectional activism, they began appearing at protests and marches around the country, clad in black skirts, shoes, tights, and pointy hats. They draped black cloth over their faces and stood in silence with signs denouncing anti-immigrant policies, supporting reproductive rights, and "hexing" white supremacy.

And thousands of witches and magic practitioners of all genders and backgrounds have come together as part of the #MagicResistance to cast spells on those in political power whose policies are harmful and destructive. They gather for monthly rituals, both in person and online, to harness their powers in an effort to ensure that the president does no harm.

Witches are powerful. They exist, and they are real. They recognize the sacred in everything, and they resist the exploitation and destruction of the earth and of humans and animals.

The system of capitalism views all aspects of the world as potential profit—it encourages competition. The system of patriarchy views men as inherently more important and powerful than non-men—it encourages dominance and hierarchy. Witches reject both systems, embracing interdependence and celebrating the power and connections of all beings.

W IS ALSO FOR . . .

WALDEN: The 1854 book by transcendentalist writer Henry David Thoreau, in which he details his time spent living in a cabin on Walden Pond in Massachusetts, and explores ideas about self-reliance, simplicity, and living outside of the norms of society.

WEDNESDAYS IN MISSISSIPPI: A little-known civil rights effort led by Dorothy Height and Polly Spiegel Cowan in the 1960s; it aimed to unite Northern and Southern women across racial, class, and religious lines.

WOBBLIES: Another name for the members of the Industrial Workers of the World, an international labor union founded in Chicago in 1905 by labor leaders like Lucy Parsons, Mother Jones, and Eugene V. Debs.

WOMEN'S INTERNATIONAL LEAGUE FOR PEACE AND FREEDOM (WILPF): A nonprofit feminist organization that has been working to unite women and end war since 1915.

MALLEUS MALEFICARUM

IN 1486 A DISCREDITED Catholic priest from Germany published a book called *Malleus Maleficarum*, which translates to "The Hammer of Witchcraft." It presented witchcraft as a grave danger to society and the church, and offered detailed instructions on how to identify and destroy suspected witches.

Malleus also lays the foundation for the assumption that witches are women. It argues that women are more likely to be witches due to their weak minds and bodies, uncontrollable sexual urges, and general evilness. The book goes to great lengths to detail the wickedness of women and specifically singles out midwives, suggesting that they're vehicles of the devil who cause diseases and eat babies. It also addresses the danger of independent women, quoting an ancient Roman author: "When a woman thinks alone, she thinks evil."

Across a span of several centuries, this wildly misogynist book was reprinted more than 30 times, and widely circulated throughout Europe (thanks to the invention of the printing press by Johannes Gutenberg). Up until the 17th century, *Malleus Maleficarum* was the second most widely read text in Europe, after the Bible—and the basis for the witch hunts that ensued. It's difficult to know how many witches were executed in Europe during the peak witch-hunting years of the 16th and 17th centuries, but most contemporary historians believe the figure is at least 50,000—and possibly far greater.

"X is for the radical histories ⋯⋯➤

How do we build a better, more just
world? → worker cooperatives, credit unions,
↑co housing, land trusts, free schools,
↑solar energy, mutual aid, rent control,
↑living wage ordinances, tenant unions,
↑community gardens, restorative
↑justice and health care for everyone ↑
↑this is what we want!!! ↑

READ: Howard Zinn, Audre Lorde, James Baldwin, Adrienne Rich, Octavia Butler, Comet + bus, Lillian Faderman

PRISON } what is
INDUSTRIAL } the school
COMPLEX } to prison pipeline
FREE MUMIA! FREE LEONARD PELTIER!

S.F. MIME TROUPE → BREAD + PUPPET THEATER → CHEAP ART!

Axis Dance Company → Ed Mock → Dance
Brigade → Contraband → Turfing → USING
OUR BODIES TO TELL STORIES ✶

Listen to → Democracy Now
and Call your Girlfriend

"LET YOUR LIFE BE A COUNTER-FRICTION
TO STOP THE MACHINE" -THOREAU

FOOD NOT BOMBS
Slow Food movement
S.F. Diggers
Food Justice
Food Deserts

LENNY BRUCE → RICHARD
PRYOR → GILDA RADNER
→ W. KAMAU BELL

DISCHORD records

FIRST WAVE SECOND WAVE THIRD WAVE

SKATE LIKE A GIRL   UNITY PAVE THE WAY

·····→ that didn't get recorded"

→ from Rad American Women a-Z

G E N E R A T I O N X X

Who writes history anyway?!?
- weather underground
- COINTELPRO
- MOVE bombing
- Helen Keller was a socialist
- Miss Ameriaca protests
- Wounded knee
- Scottsboro boys → Emmett Till → central park five

BAYARD RUSTIN ⇒ The 1963 MARCH ON WASHINGTON WAS ORGANIZED BY AN OPENLY GAY MAN

Who built the railroads?
Why doesn't Flint have clean water?
Why did we fight in Vietnam and Iraq?
→ Who profits from War?
Why are there so many unhoused people in my city?

She wore a tunic that said "PEACE PILGRIM" FROM 1953-1981 Peace Pilgrim walked 25,000 miles in the United States talking to people about PEACE.

DECOLONIZE

RESEARCH
Buffalo soldiers
Tuskeegee Airmen
WACs
Hush Habbors

Henrietta Lacks
Rosewood massacre

SILENCE = DEATH
ACT UP

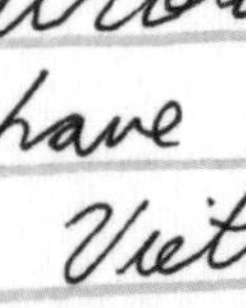

PEACE PILGRIM

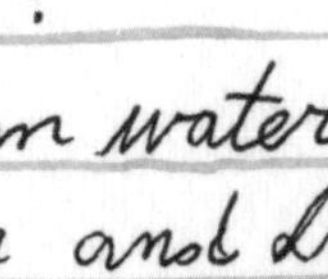

TOYPURINA
1760-1799

Proletarian, Funkadelic;
Parliamentarian, Pro Revolt
in the 21st Centurian → THE COUP

Y

IS FOR

YOUTH CLIMATE MOVEMENT

THE YOUNG LEADERS WORKING TO PROTECT OUR PLANET

"This isn't just climate change anymore—it's climate chaos. This isn't just global warming—it's global catastrophe."
—SAMANTHA MAY, AGE 12, CLIMATE ACTIVIST

CLIMATE CHANGE IS REAL. It's happening. And we need to act—*now*. That is the core message of the Youth Climate Movement, a growing network of young activists and organizations leading the urgent fight to address and reverse climate change across the United States and around the world.

The majority of scientists agree that human contributions to the greenhouse effect are the root cause of the widespread changes our climate is experiencing. Gases in the atmosphere, such as CO2 and methane, trap heat and then prevent its escape from the planet. This heat causes an increase in surface temperatures—new heat records are being set almost every year. It destabilizes weather patterns around the globe, causing more catastrophic weather events, including hurricanes, extreme storms and rainfall, droughts and heat waves, and resulting floods and forest fires. In the last century alone, global sea levels have risen 6.7 inches—and in the next 100 years, some scientists suggest they could rise as much as 4 feet.

When it comes to taking action on climate change, world leaders tend to debate, deny, or delay. The Youth Climate Movement believes we can't wait. They press forward, leading strikes and marches, confronting their elected officials, and educating their peers about what it will take to ensure a healthy planet and future.

This story is about Americans who want to ensure that we get to have that future. It's told mostly in their voices, because they have something important to say—and we need to listen.

STANDING ROCK 2014

IN 2014, A LARGE energy corporation wanted to build a huge underground oil pipeline from North Dakota to Illinois. The Dakota Access Pipeline (DAPL) would move half a million barrels of oil per day—and be built directly beneath land, rivers, and burial grounds that are sacred to numerous indigenous Native people, including those living on the Standing Rock Sioux reservation.

While the corporation argued that the pipeline would be safe, the indigenous communities knew the truth: pipeline accidents will inevitably occur, and when they do, the damage can be irreversible, toxic, and deadly. The indigenous people of the region decided to take a stand to protect their land—and it was the youth who took the lead, setting up camps and holding ceremonies.

Using the hashtags #NoDAPL, #mniwiconi, #WaterIsLife, and #StandWithStandingRock, they used social media to spread the message that the pipeline threatened more than the purity of their drinking water—it threatened their health, their culture, and their lives. It was also, they knew, one part of a much larger environmental crisis that their generation is going to inherit—and that their generation must fix. Members of hundreds of Native tribes came to Standing Rock to show solidarity for the people and the earth, and thousands of nonnatives joined the demonstrations too.

"It's important to know that, for Native and indigenous people, this is not just about protecting the climate, the land, and the water so that we can *survive*. It's deeply connected to *who we are*—the natural world is our culture. We've been preaching this and valuing these sacred resources since the beginning of time. Due to this, indigenous people should be represented with all climate actions.

"The United States has a long history of extracting natural resources from indigenous lands. We tend to live in rural areas, which is where most of our reservations or ancestral lands are, and these regions often have the valuable resources they want. When massive oil pipelines are built through indigenous land, it's not only a threat to our environment, but also to our culture. It's a double whammy. This happens throughout the world: wherever resources are being extracted, whether it's oil, water, or trees, you can guarantee an indigenous community lives nearby.

"The Dakota Access Pipeline was being built through unceded Sioux territory. The construction is a direct violation of the Treaty of Fort Laramie of April 29, 1868, also known as the Sioux Treaty, which gave the Sioux people sovereign control over the land.

"The International Indigenous Youth Council started to address this in 2016, armed with the knowledge of our culture and historical contexts. We have to protect our women, our land, our culture. We ask the world, and the corporations, to please honor our treaties, our rights, and our livelihoods.

"We are led by young women and two-spirit people (for us, "two spirit" is someone whose energy encapsulates both masculine and feminine qualities).

"There is a basic understanding among many first nations that our behaviors are the result of actions, thoughts, and prayers that go back seven generations, and that whatever we do, think, and pray about will impact the future seven generations. There is a prophecy among several Native tribes that says seven generations after contact with Europeans there will be a great awakening among Indigenous tribes and allies. Through this awakening people from all over the world would stand together to save Turtle Island [a term for Earth]. *We are the seventh generation. It's happening now—the prophecy is coming true."*

—MEREYA GOETZINGER-BLANCO, MEMBER OF THE INTERNATIONAL INDIGENOUS YOUTH COUNCIL

JULIANA V. UNITED STATES
2015

IN 2015 A GROUP of 21 young people filed a lawsuit against the United States government, asserting that the government's failure to address climate change is a violation of their constitutional rights to life, liberty, and happiness. Climate activist Kelsey Juliana is the named plaintiff on the case, titled *Juliana v. United States*.

"I began climate activism at age 10. It became my life—all my school projects became ways to learn more about climate change. After 8th grade, I filed a case against the state of Oregon, and that's how I began climate litigation. It was a snowball effect: I wanted to hold my school accountable for climate change, then my city, then the state . . . and now I want to hold the federal government accountable.

"When I was in 8th grade, no one else seemed to care about climate change. Now there are 21 of us suing the federal government. We're not scientists or lawyers or experts. We're individual young people being called to collectively take on the greatest challenge of our time. We are trying to hold the systems of power accountable."

—KELSEY JULIANA, AGE 23, LEAD PLAINTIFF

2018 YOUTH CLIMATE MARCH

ON JULY 21, 2018, thousands of students across America marched for climate justice in Washington, DC, and in 25 cities around the world. The idea for the first Youth Climate March came from Jamie Margolin, whose inspiration to become a climate activist came, in part, from witnessing the efforts of the Standing Rock activists.

"For a long time, I was just a kid who learned about climate change. I cared about it, but it was so scary to me. I didn't know what to do with that fear. Whenever a news story about climate change came on, I would turn it off. That all changed with the 2016 election.

"I realized that I had to take this fear and channel it into something productive. I watched a documentary about the Standing Rock activists, and was so moved by the way these indigenous youth from a really disadvantaged community have managed to start this international movement. I thought if they could do it under those circumstances, I could do it too.

"During the summer of 2017, I had the idea: What if there was a youth climate march? I imagined a big event that would put the world's eyes on youth climate activism. I posted on Instagram and got a few responses from young people who wanted to help, from across the country. We formed a team and for an entire year we organized, and a year later, on July 21, 2018, we had the Youth Climate March on Washington and in 25 cities around the world.

"We're called Zero Hour because *this* is 'zero hour' to work on climate change. Anything other than immediate action now is denying it and dooming life on earth. There's no gray area on survival— either we survive this or we don't."

—JAMIE MARGOLIN, AGE 18, FOUNDER OF ZERO HOUR

IN AUGUST 2018, a 15-year-old Swedish teenager named Greta Thunberg began her *skolstrejk för klimatet* (school strike for climate) when she started skipping school to demand action on climate change by protesting outside of the Swedish Parliament building. She quickly inspired young people around the world to do the same. On March 15, 2019, more than one million students in 125 countries went on strike to bring attention to climate change. In New York City, 12-year-old Alexandria Villaseñor began striking outside of the United Nations headquarters every Friday.

"I was visiting family in Davis, California, in November of 2018 when the Paradise Fire broke out. I was an hour away from the fire, but we had the worst air quality in the world at the time. The smoke was so terrible, it was seeping into the house.

"I made the connection that climate change *is* fueling California's wildfires, and making them more extreme. California's fire season is all year round now. I started researching climate change and paying attention to the United Nations Climate Change Conference. I was hoping that world leaders would come to an agreement to reduce greenhouse gas emissions by 2030, but when they didn't, I got really mad.

"Then I saw Greta Thunberg speak. On December 14, 2018, I started my own school strike for climate at the United Nations headquarters in New York City. I've been on strike for 22 weeks now (as of yesterday). Students all over the world are taking direct action, going out into the streets every Friday to strike. We ARE starting to make change.

"I want to get climate education into schools so we can start learning the facts. Climate change is not an opinion— it's science."

—ALEXANDRIA VILLASEÑOR, AGE 13, FOUNDER OF EARTH UPRISING

YOUTH VS. APOCALYPSE IS a diverse group of young climate justice activists working together to lift the voices of youth— especially youth of color—and to fight for a livable climate and a sustainable, just world. In 2019 several members of Youth vs. Apocalypse joined members of the climate justice group the Sunrise Movement in a visit to the office of California Senator Dianne Feinstein. Their tense interaction went viral when Senator Feinstein seemed to dismiss their concerns about climate change and the Green New Deal, an ambitious legislative plan to address climate change and create new jobs.

"I got started with climate activism when I was 13 years old and I was invited to an action by a friend. We went to deliver a letter to a local developer who was trying to build a coal terminal through my neighborhood in West Oakland, California. It would have severely impacted the lives and health of people that I know and love.

"To be honest, before I got involved in the climate movement, I disregarded it. I saw it as a 'white issue'—like, who has time to save the rainforests when black people are being shot by police every day? Then I realized that climate injustice is rooted in our culture of greed and exploitation. That coal terminal awakened me to the reality of the climate movement.

"Our culture is realizing that climate change is really important. People my age are actually caring, and wanting to do something about it. We've seen people in power implement plans that haven't worked. We have that whole story behind us, and we can look to the past to analyze how best to move forward."

—ISHA CLARKE, AGE 16, YOUTH VS. APOCALYPSE

"I like to go for a straightforward approach when I give speeches to grown-ups: I tell them climate change is gonna kill us. How can we let it happen? We have to let the Green New Deal pass. I spoke with representatives from the Environmental Protection Agency. I told them they need to protect the youth.

"I feel empowered: when I'm speaking, it's the adults looking to learn from *us* about what they can do to help.

"A lot of people say I should be a politician. Even my mom said she thinks I'm going to be president. But I don't want to be in charge of a group of people—I want to be *with* people, guiding them instead of directing them."

—SAMANTHA MAY, AGE 12, YOUTH VS. APOCALYPSE

Y ALSO FOR . . .

YELLOW POWER: A term used in the 1960s and '70s to refer to the new Asian American civil rights movement.

YIPPIES: The members of the Youth International Party, founded in 1967, an offshoot of the free speech and antiwar movements.

YOUNG LORDS: A national organization, inspired by the Black Panthers, that championed liberation, self-determination, and justice for Puerto Rican and Latinx people in the late 1960s to mid-1970s.

IS FOR
ZUCCOTTI PARK

AND THE OCCUPY MOVEMENT THAT MOBILIZED THE 99 PERCENT

IF YOU WALKED PAST Zuccotti Park on an average day, you probably wouldn't think much of it. As New York City parks go, it's fairly unremarkable. It's not massive Central Park, or busy Union Square. There's no giant playground, no big green lawn. Located in Lower Manhattan, blocks from the southernmost tip of the island, Zuccotti is a mostly concrete plaza with some trees and a number of shiny granite benches for sitting. In the mornings, people sit on the benches, drinking coffee and reading the paper. At night it's mostly empty: the trees are illuminated, and the skyscrapers that surround the park light up the night.

But if you'd walked by Zuccotti Park in the fall of 2011, you'd have seen—and heard—something very different. There were tents, hundreds of them, packed together to make a pop-up city, including a kitchen, a library, a children's area, and a work station. You would have heard hundreds, even thousands, of people gathered together talking, dancing, drumming, chanting, and debating. They held massive meetings without microphones, using hand signals and their own collective voices to share ideas and opinions. You'd have seen the police, and bicycles, and news crews; cameras, celebrities, politicians, and college students. There were marches and rallies, banners and signs. And you almost certainly would have heard someone chanting this declaration: "We are the 99 percent!"

This was Occupy Wall Street, a social and political movement that began with a small group of activists who decided to "occupy" a public space to draw attention to some of the 21st century's most pressing issues, including corporate power and the widening gap between the rich—and everyone else. Despite having no formal leader and no one single demand, the Occupy movement quickly grew into a worldwide phenomenon. And it all started there, in Zuccotti Park.

THE PARK ITSELF MAY not be remarkable, but its location and history are. It sits in the midst of Wall Street, the center of America's financial and banking industry. It's where some of the world's richest, most powerful men and women do business every day, buying, selling, and trading stocks and making decisions that shape the global economy.

It's also one block from another significant site: the former location of the World Trade

Center, also known as the Twin Towers, which stood higher than any other New York City skyscrapers until they were destroyed in a terrorist attack on September 11, 2001. Nearly three thousand people died that day, and Zuccotti Park was completely covered in ash and debris. It became an important staging ground for rescue and recovery operations.

But beyond that, Zuccotti is located in an area that has long been a site of resistance and rebellion. The name "Wall Street" likely comes from an actual barricade that Dutch settlers built to keep Native Americans, pirates, and British colonists out. It's where a major slave revolt took place in 1710, and where New York City's main slave market opened the following year. In 1773 massive crowds gathered there to protest the Tea Act, just weeks before the Boston Tea Party. It's where George Washington was inaugurated, where the Bill of Rights was passed, and where founding father Alexander Hamilton is buried.

Once Wall Street became a center of financial power, it was the target of numerous protests, from the unemployed demanding help during the Panic of 1857 (an early financial crisis triggered by a decrease in Europe's purchasing of American agricultural exports) to the still-unsolved 1920 bombing of J. P. Morgan bank by an unknown group of anarchists. So while the 21st-century bankers and businesspeople weren't used to seeing protesters in their midst, it wasn't the first time that Americans had gathered in the area to demand some kind of change.

OCCUPY ACTIVISTS WANTED TO draw attention to how the rich keep getting richer: since the 1970s, the top 1 percent of Americans have gotten richer, while the rest of the wage-earners in the country—"the 99 percent"—have not. And that 1 percent of the population holds almost 50 percent of the wealth in the country. During the first decade of the 21st century, some corporate CEOs were making in *one day* what public school teachers made in an *entire year*. In many cities, hard-working people could barely afford rent, while a tiny percentage of the population just kept making more money.

Protesters were also reacting to the financial crisis of 2008, America's worst financial crisis since the stock market crash of 1929 that preceded the Great Depression. The recent crisis was mostly due to problems within the banking industry, which had been offering people loans that they couldn't repay. Many loans came with a monthly payment that increased after the first two or three years of the loan, often increasing so high that people could no longer afford the loan. When they were unable to pay, they lost their homes to a process called foreclosure and had to move out.

For three years, from 2008 to 2011, during both the Bush and Obama administrations, the Treasury and the central bank of the United States, the Federal Reserve, worked to prevent a collapse of the banking system and to shore it up. While this bailout likely did prevent an extreme global financial disaster, it also angered many people who felt that money should instead go to ordinary Americans who were suffering through this Great Recession, and not the corporations that had profited from and caused the problem in the first place.

These concerns about the class divide in America were not new, but by 2011 they had taken on a new, 21st-century feel. Social media sites like Twitter and Facebook now allowed activists to spread their messages and share events with the world. And that's pretty much how Occupy happened. In July 2011, the editors of an anticonsumer-ist magazine called *AdBusters* used social media to spread the word about a public protest on Wall Street: the announce-ment was an image of a ballerina doing a pirouette on top of the Charging Bull statue that stands in New York's Financial District, a symbol of American money and power. Below the bull were the words *#OccupyWallStreet. September 17th. Bring tent.* (The date was the birthday of one of the organizer's mothers.) During the next few months, the announcement was shared thousands of times. A loose-knit group of about 200 people worked to plan the logistics, and during one planning meeting, an organizer used the phrase "the 1 percent" to talk about the richest peo-ple in America. "*We* are the 99 percent," he said. The phrase caught on, and soon it was the movement's rallying cry.

ON SEPTEMBER 17, 2011—ten years and one week after the September 11, 2001, tragedy—several hundred energized people marched into Lower Manhattan to set up their tents. They had many demands and concerns, from eco-nomic to environmental to social justice, and they rejected individual leadership, preferring instead to work together as a collective. Some have referred to Occupy as a "leaderless" movement, because there was no one single person in charge. Others prefer the term "leader-full movement," implying that there were *many* leaders who all worked together.

These leaders developed a decision-making process called a General Assembly, or GA, that allowed everyone to participate equally. The GAs were big group meetings, held almost nightly, where ideas were shared and decisions were made. Anyone could submit an idea or proposal to be shared with the group. Then people broke into small groups to discuss and debate the idea. Nearly everyone would need to agree on a plan for it to be approved.

During that first week there wasn't much media coverage—most New Yorkers were still trying to figure out what, exactly, was going on down at Zuccotti Park. But the movement didn't need traditional media coverage to get the message out: #Occupy and #OccupyWallStreet were all over social media. More and more people came down to Lower Manhattan to check it out—and many of them ended up staying. The atmosphere of energy and spirit was infectious. And after two huge marches (including one that brought thousands of protesters to the Brooklyn Bridge) resulted in a police crackdown and hundreds of arrests, the media started paying attention.

By then, Occupy was everywhere. The movement, the idea, the phrase was spreading. In more than 100 cities across the country, people were coming together and gathering in public spaces to hold GAs, organize marches, set up encampments, and discuss ways to address inequality both nationally and in their own communities. There were Occupy camps in big cities, such as Chicago, Los Angeles, Kansas City, Honolulu, and Memphis, as well as smaller ones, from Norman, Oklahoma, to Ames, Iowa. By October, there were Occupy groups in almost every state, and on college campuses from Harvard to Ohio State. Soon Occupy was international, with groups in Tokyo, Milan, Sydney, and Algiers. One month after the Zuccotti camp was established, more than 900 cities around the world held simultaneous protests to address global inequalities.

As the Zuccotti encampment grew and it became clear that they weren't going to go away, the city—and the police—grew less supportive. They cited concerns about public safety and sanitation and regularly threatened to evict the camp. But then a volunteer lawyer discovered something very interesting about Zuccotti Park: due to an obscure legal loophole, the park was public, meaning it was open to anyone—but it was privately owned by a real estate company. This meant that, unlike most city parks, it had no official closing time. Legally, Zuccotti Park was open 24 hours a day, and anyone had a legal right to be there. The police could continue to monitor the park and arrest people during marches, but for the time being, the Zuccotti camp could legally remain—for a while.

As winter came, the weather shifted. Many camps across the country ended voluntarily because of weather conditions, and because people felt they'd made their point. In mid-November, two months after it started, the camp at Zuccotti Park was finally evicted. The tents came down—but the movement didn't end.

MANY HAVE ASKED WHETHER Occupy *accomplished* anything. All those people camping in those public spaces, marching and chanting and holding meetings: What did they actually *do*? It can be hard to determine the specific impacts of a movement like Occupy.

At the end of 2011, *TIME* magazine declared "The Protester" to be the Person of the Year, devoting the issue to stories and images from the US and around the world. It asserted that 2011 was unique, comparing it to 1989 (the year the Berlin Wall fell) and 1968 (the year of massive social change and anti–Vietnam War protests in the US and abroad), "but more extraordinary, more global, more democratic."

In the US alone, millions of people were exposed to protest and to new ideas in ways they'd perhaps never been before. People heard about Occupy, they saw coverage of it, and they heard participants talk about income inequality, housing instability, injustice, corporate control of politics, and more.

Occupy may have ended, but it had—and still has—a big impact on the national conversation about wealth distribution and corporate power. The 99 percent and the 1 percent have become familiar phrases, and have changed the way politicians talk about wealth and class. The ideals behind Occupy have impacted elections, actions, and multiple movements, including the Fight for $15 movement to raise the minimum wage, the movement to eliminate student debt, and the movement to halt climate change.

Z IS ALSO FOR . . .

ZINE: A self-published mini magazine or book with a modest circulation, usually made by an individual or small group on a photocopy machine. Zines often reflect the interests and ideas of a specific subculture. The term can be traced to the 1930s, when readers of popular science-fiction series created fanzines to share ideas about characters and stories. Zines have been a key part of the communication and development of underground cultures ever since, from the Beat Generation and counterculture movements of the 1950s and '60s to the Riot Grrrl, punk, queer, and skateboarding cultures of the 1980s and '90s to 21st-century zines reflecting a wide variety of political and social issues.

ZOOT SUIT: A highly stylized men's suit popular in the 1930s and '40s and worn primarily by African American and Latino men in working-class parts of Los Angeles and Harlem; those wearing the suits were often targets of harassment, arrest, and assault. Zoot suits became a symbol of cultural pride and resistance.

NOTES ON THE ILLUSTRATIONS

The art in *Rad American History A–Z* is original papercuts and watercolors by Miriam Klein Stahl. Following are descriptions of select images.

Page 4: Two Alcatraz occupiers, Oohosis (left) and Sandy Berger (right)

Page 10: #BlackLivesMatter founders (left to right) Opal Tometi, Alicia Garza, and Patrisse Cullors, in front of generations of civil rights and racial justice activists

Page 16: Harriet Tubman and the Combahee River

Page 21: Members of the Combahee River Collective marching in Boston in 1970

Page 22: Lucretia Mott and the Declaration of Sentiments

Page 28: Judi Bari and the redwoods

Page 30: Earth First! logo

Page 34: Art based on WPA poster imagery

Page 39: 1937 promotional poster for "Revolt of the Beavers"

Page 40: White pine tree with eagle set against traditional Iroquois wampum belt

Page 42: Traditional Iroquois longhouse

Page 46: Hull House, based on a 1910 postcard

Page 49: Jane Addams (left) and Ellen Gates Starr (right)

Page 52: Ed Roberts (left) and Don Galloway (right) on Telegraph Avenue in Berkeley, California

Page 55: Judy Heumann

Page 58: Billie Holiday

Page 64: Japanese-owned business in Oakland, California, just before the owner was forced into a prison camp in March 1942; based on a photograph by Dorothea Lange

Page 67: Fred Korematsu

Page 70: Library books in front of a card catalog

Page 74: Carla Hayden

Page 75: The first Carnegie Library in the US, built in 1888 in Braddock, Pennsylvania

Page 76: 2017 Women's March

Page 79: 1917 NAACP Silent Parade

Page 82: Dr. Martin Luther King Jr. walking with children in Birmingham, Alabama

Page 84: 2018 March for Our Lives speakers (left to right) Edna Chavez, Emma Gonzalez, and Naomi Wadler

Page 86: The toxic debris, smoke, and water vapor from a nuclear bomb detonation, called a mushroom cloud

Page 89: Flyer for the St. Louis Baby Tooth Survey (circa 1950s)

Page 92: Cover of the 1971 edition of *Our Bodies, Ourselves*

Page 95: The founding members of the Boston Women's Health Book Collective (1976)

Page 98: Sister Corita in her studio

Page 104: The AIDS quilt displayed on the National Mall in Washington, DC

ACKNOWLEDGMENTS

As always, we thank our friends, colleagues, and families, who sustain, love, and support us.

The Ten Speed Press team, who give us the space to put radical work into the world. Charlotte and Steven, who advocate and root for us.

Mia Eichel and Ayame Keane-Lee, for being invaluable research assistants.

Professor Thanayi Jackson, Professor Larissa Mercado-López, Jason Pontius, and Leslie Van Every, for being brilliant outside readers with clear, critical eyes.

A big thank you to Lena Wolff for encouraging an expanded art form and for sharing her studio space, and the Sullivan family for the space, time, and snacks.

The following people provided input, advice, and support during the early stages of this book, truly helping to shape and guide it:

Amy Sonnie, Andrea Yee, Angela Moffett, Anoop Mirpuri, Caterina Meyers, Catherine Newman, Constance Moore, Debra Michals, Erika Mailman, Hindatu Mohammed, Innosanto Nagara, James Costello, Jennifer Ruby, Julie Scelfo, Julie Shayne, Kati Dombrosky, Lauren Pariani, Leslie Tolf, Lisa Vallejos, Mary Roach, Matthew Zapruder, Nina Portugal, Rachel-Anne Palacios, Ray Black, Rebecca Skloot, Rob Waters, Shannon Erby, Stephanie Piper, and W. Kamau Bell

Enormous gratitude to the following people, who offered invaluable feedback, critique, stories, and information, often speaking and corresponding with us at length as we crafted and edited each story and picture.

Thank you for your time, generosity, and scholarship:

Adam Mansbach, Alexandria Villaseñor and family, Alicia Garza, Amanda Yates Garcia, Anna Tamura, Annie Anderson, Anya Jabour, Ashley Farmer, Barbara Schatz, Barbara Smith, Bridie Lee, Bruce Johansen, Carol Faulkner, Carolyn Norr, Cava Menzies, Cleve Jones, Corin Tucker, Daniela Sea, David Solnit, Dori Midnight, Dunstan Bruce, Emily Klein, Eric Reiss, Innosanto Nagara, Isha Clarke, Jamie Margolin, Jane Pincus, Jasilyn Charger, Jen Smith, Jennifer Burek Pierce, Jennifer Lutzenberger Phillips, Jenny Schmidt, Joan Ditzion, Josh Healey, Judy Norsigian, Karen Korematsu, Kelsey Juliana, LaNada War Jack, Laura Atkins, Laura Belmonte, LeRoy Hill and the Haudenosaunee Confederacy, Lisa Tetrault, Maegan Parker Brooks, Mark Stryker, Martha Olney, Mereya Goetzinger-Blanco, Mia Bonta, Michael M. Hughes, Michelle Tea, Nikki McClure, Noelani Goodyear, *Our Bodies, Ourselves* founders, Representative Rob Bonta, Samantha May, Sara Marcus, Sherrie Tucker, Stan Yogi, Stuart James, Susan Zakin, Tammy Rae Carland, Thomas Gregory, Tokata Iron Eyes, Tony Uranday, and Wayne Wiegand

Note: We consulted with many brilliant individuals who helped us immensely in the writing of this book. However, please know that any errors, factual or otherwise, are ours. We welcome feedback and will do what we can to make corrections in future editions.

For more information, a selected bibliography, and additional resources, please visit www.radamericanhistory.com

DEDICATION

This book is dedicated to the historians, librarians, educators, activists, freedom fighters, workers, scholars, radicals—and you.

And also, as always, to our children—Ivy and Benson, and Hazel.

ABOUT THE AUTHOR AND ILLUSTRATOR

Kate Schatz and Miriam Klein Stahl are the author and illustrator of the *New York Times* bestselling books *Rad American Women A–Z* and *Rad Women Worldwide,* as well as *Rad Girls Can* and *My Rad Life: A Journal.* They are artists, educators, activists, and history geeks who dream of and work toward a just, feminist, and rad future for all. They live in the San Francisco Bay Area with their families and pets.

Miriam's papercut illustrations are created using paper, pencil, and an X-Acto knife. Background paintings are done using watercolors.

INDEX

Published in the United States by Ten Speed Press, an imprint
of Random House, a division of Penguin Random House LLC,
New York.

www.tenspeed.com

Ten Speed Press and the Ten Speed Press colophon are registered
trademarks of Penguin Random House LLC.

Library of Congress Cataloging-in-Publication Data is on file with
the publisher.

Hardcover ISBN: 978-1-9848-5683-8
eBook ISBN: 978-1-9848-5684-5

Printed in China

Design by Lizzie Allen

10 9 8 7 6 5 4 3 2 1

First Edition

1942
Executive Order 9066 leads to mass incarceration of Japanese Americans

1944
Supreme Court hears *Korematsu v. United States*

Congress passes G.I. Bill of Rights

1945
US drops nuclear bombs on Hiroshima and Nagasaki

World War II ends

1947
Cold War begins

1950
Mattachine Society is founded

1952
The Immigration and Nationality Act passes, allowing people of Asian descent to become naturalized citizens

1971
Occupation of Alcatraz ends

1970
Gay Liberation Front holds the first gay pride march

UFW is recognized as a legitimate union

President Nixon ends Native American termination policy

Boston Women's Health Collective prints first version of *Our Bodies, Ourselves*

1969
Occupation of Alcatraz begins

Stonewall raid

First Female Liberation Conference

1968
Dr. Martin Luther King Jr. is assassinated

Bobby Kennedy is assassinated

Chicano Blowouts

Cesar Chavez goes on hunger strike

First W.I.T.C.H. action

Third World Liberation Front strikes

American track stars raise fists at the Olympics

1966
The National Organization for Women is founded

Vanguard Street Sweep

Gee's Bend quilters form the Freedom Quilting Bee

Black Panthers is founded

1965
US enters Vietnam War

Selma to Montgomery March

Voting Rights Act signed into law

Dewey's lunch counter sit-ins

AWOC and NFWA join to create the United Farm Workers Organizing Committee (UFW)

Malcolm X is assassinated

1972
First Center for Independent Living opens

1973
Roe v. Wade is decided

Paris Peace Accords ends US involvement in Vietnam War

1974
Combahee River Collective is founded

1976
Ed Roberts is appointed director of the California Department of Vocational Rehabilitation

President Ford rescinds Executive Order 9066

1977
Section 504 protests lead to enforcement of landmark disability rights

1981
First recognized cases of AIDS

Earth First! is founded

2018
Marjory Stoneman Douglas high school shooting

March for Our Lives protest

Youth Climate March

#MeToo movement goes viral

2017
Women's March

2016
Colin Kaepernick takes a knee during the national anthem

Hillary Rodham Clinton is the first woman to run for president as the Democratic nominee

2015
Obergefell v. Hodges legalizes gay marriage

Dakota Access Pipeline protests

2013
#BlackLivesMatter is founded